THE PROSPEROUS SEED

Dwayne Norman

Empyrion Publishing
Winter Garden FL 34778
EmpyrionPublishing.com

The Prosperous Seed

Copyright © 2015 by Dwayne Norman
ISBN: 978-0692594216

Empyrion Publishing
PO Box 784327
Winter Garden, FL
Info@EmpyrionPublishing.com

Unless otherwise noted, all Scripture quotations are from the New King James Version.

Printed in the United States of America

CONTENTS

CHAPTER
1

GOD ONLY WANTS
GOOD FOR YOU

If you are born again, your Heavenly Father wants to lavish you with good gifts from Heaven. He loves you as much as He loves Jesus (John 17:23). He only wants good for you! Expect to experience God's best for you and your family! In the Good News Bible, Jeremiah 29:11, 12 says:

"I alone know the plans I have for you, plans to bring you prosperity and not disaster, plans to bring about the future you hope for.
Then you will call to me. You will come and pray to me, and I will answer you."

So, those are God's plans for <u>You</u>! Only blessings, health, peace, wisdom and life more abundantly (John 10:10)! My recommendation is to take God's offer. Don't buck and resist what your Heavenly Father wants to do for you! Now listen, we are going to talk about financing God's Kingdom in a little while, but first, God wants <u>you</u> blessed! How can you pay to send the Gospel into every nation if you are broke? Wouldn't you like to pay another Believer's house payment of $1,000? How you can do that if all you have is $5.00? Whether you realize this or not, you have to be blessed (I don't just mean as a good confession, but in manifestation-money in the bank blessed) to be a blessing to others.

Let me ask you this question. How do you receive healing and how do you maintain walking in perfect health? You do it by faith in God don't you? You spend time meditating and hearing God's Word on the subject of healing. When you do that, your faith will grow stronger and stronger. It takes time doesn't it? But it is well worth it. You and I have to do the same thing when it comes to prospering financially. We must develop our faith in the area of finances, especially in sowing and reaping. Always remember that faith works the same way in every realm. Walking and living by faith is the only way to please God (Hebrews 11:6). Everything we receive from the Lord is through faith. If you get a chance, read our book "Just Believe" it will be a great blessing to you in your walk of faith. You and I need to be totally convinced of how much God loves us and that His heart towards us is always for good. Matthew 7:9-11 tells us:

"Or what man is there among you who, if his son asks for bread, will give him a stone? Or if he asks for a fish, will he give him a serpent?

If you then, being evil, know how to give good gifts to your children, <u>how much more</u> will your Father who is in heaven give good things to those who ask Him!"

If you have children (my wife and I have four), you don't want them to experience anything bad in their lives, do you? If they didn't have shoes to wear, all of their clothes had holes in them and they had to walk everywhere, would that please you? Would that give you great pleasure? Of course not! Well let's be just as intelligent when it comes to pleasing our Heavenly Father. If your child came to you and said, "Mom and Dad, I have taken a vow of poverty, to be broke and sick for the rest of my life; because I know how much that pleases you. I know by doing this I will be more humble and spiritual in your eyes." What would you say to that? You would probably say that's the dumbest thing I've ever heard? Wouldn't you be very disappointed that <u>your</u> children believe that way? You would probably question them as to why they said such a thing. You would be totally amazed that they actually thought poverty and sickness are your will for them. I feel confident that you would immediately correct them on their thinking, and question them as to how they came up with such preposterous ideas. Now listen closely. You should be just as shocked when you hear ministers say that sickness and poverty glorify God!

I hope you see where I am going with this. Most of the Church, I mean God's very own sons and daughters have taught this. By listening to unscriptural teaching, they actually believe that poverty and sickness are signs of humility and spirituality. They really believe they are pleasing God through disease and financial lack, and they are as far from Biblical truth as the east is from the west! Yet, they will pray for God to use them in financing the Gospel throughout the earth. Well how are they going to do that without any money? Come on, let's use our brains here! If you really believe that your sickness is God's will, then why are you going to the doctor and taking medicine? It seems to me you are trying to get out of His will, if you really believed it was His will for you to be sick. If you truly believed that having money and things are unspiritual, then why do you go to work every day? Why don't you quit your job so you can be really "spiritual"? Wouldn't that be the logical conclusion, if you truly believed that God did not want you to prosper?

Many Christians have one way they live and believe outside the church, and another way inside the church. We need to go to the source of Truth (John

17:17), learn God's Word (not man's religion) and live by it every day. The devil has fed the Church a load of lies, and we would not have believed it had we examined everything we were taught in light of the Word of God. God's Word should always be our final authority! So, let's go to God's Word! Even if a minister prophesies to you, his word should never override God's Word if he is genuinely hearing from the Lord. The Spirit of God and His Word always agree (I John 5:7); therefore, if we are being led by the Holy Spirit, it will always line up with the Word of God!

I want you to be totally convinced of how much God desires for you to experience all of His blessings. He wants you to be completely debt free and abounding in prosperity. He wants you to be a huge financial channel that He can use to finance the Gospel into every nation. You may be thinking why do I need to be so convinced? Because faith can only be released where the will of God is known, and remember, it takes faith to receive from the Lord. Yes, it is very true that God has already finished and completed everything for us in Christ, but we must operate in faith to make withdrawals from our Heavenly account. We still have to use our faith to receive the manifestation of all that Jesus finished for us. Jesus saved and healed us at Calvary, but we still have to operate in faith to experience those blessings. We still have to accept

Jesus as our Lord and Savior for salvation to become real in our lives. The same goes for healing, deliverance, prosperity, joy, peace, wisdom and every other blessing. Even though everything is finished by God's grace, it does not automatically materialize in our lives. We have to trust God and expect (by faith) what He has done for us (through Jesus' death and resurrection) to come to pass in our lives. We need to learn how to be good receivers as well as good givers.

How do we learn what God's will is concerning our finances? The same way we learned what His will was concerning our salvation and healing; through His Word. God's Word is His will for man (II Timothy 3:16, 17). So, now I want us to go to the very beginning, where God made known His will concerning man's prosperity. Genesis 1:27, 28; 2:8-12 says,

"So God created man in His own image; in the image of God He created him; male and female He created them.

Then God blessed them, and God said to them, 'Be fruitful and multiply; fill the earth and subdue it; have dominion over the fish of the sea, over the birds of the air, and over every living thing that moves on the earth.'"

"The Lord God planted a garden eastward in Eden, and there He put the man whom He had formed.

And out of the ground the Lord God made every tree grow that is pleasant to the sight and good for food. The tree of life was also in the midst of the garden, and the tree of the knowledge of good and evil.

Now a river went out of Eden to water the garden, and from there it parted and became four riverheads.

The name of the first is Pishon; it is the one which skirts the whole land of Havilah, where there is <u>gold.</u>

And the gold of that land is good. Bdellium and onyx stone are there."

Since God's word reveals His will to man, I want to show you several more Scriptures to convince you that God strongly desires (or wills) for you to be very prosperous and a great blessing to others. After reading these verses in Genesis, I want to ask you a question. Why did God want Adam and Eve to be fruitful or prosperous, to take dominion and subdue the earth? Why did He want them and of course all of their children to rule and reign as kings in life? Why did God give them plenty of gold and precious stones? Why did God bless them with an abundance of material blessings? Notice, I did not say spiritual blessings. I said material blessings. If your answer is to tithe to their church, to feed the poor, to finance the Gospel and to win the lost to Jesus, you would be totally wrong. Well isn't that important for Believers to do? <u>Yes, and let me say a hundred times yes</u>!! That is one of the main things the Church should be engaged in today!

But, God blessed Adam and Eve, gave them an abundance of gold, great material prosperity and told them to take dominion (that means to rule and reign) <u>before they ever sinned</u>. The Lord told them this before they ate of the fruit of the tree and died spiritually. You may be thinking why is that important? Well, before man sinned there were not any lost people to get saved, not any poor to feed, not any churches and traveling ministries to support and there was not any curse on the earth. So, let me ask you again. Why did God <u>originally</u> bless man? I know you are thinking it, and it's ok to say it. If Adam and Eve had never sinned, then the only reason for God creating all of the good things (not just spiritual, but material) on this earth was for His children to **enjoy**. Did you catch that word? Enjoy! That is still God's will today! God's will has never changed when it comes to His children enjoying His blessings and goodness in their lives.

Now, after man sinned, God had to add some things to His original intention for man. He had to give His people some further instructions. He gave us some new orders didn't He? As God's family and the body of Christ, we have been sent to this earth to fulfill the Great Commission (Mark 16:15-20) and preach the Gospel through out every nation. You might say we are missionaries from Heaven. But while we are carrying out this Great Commission let's not forget that it did not exist before Adam sinned; therefore, it is still God's will for His children to enjoy all of His blessings. Our Father longs for us to enjoy His blessings and to have plenty to give to every good work (II Corinthians 9:8). God's blessings in our lives are also for a testimony to the world. The world should look at the Church and say, "They must be the blessed of the Lord. Their God must really be God. Their God must really love them!" I don't mean that we have to tell them to say that. They should voluntarily say that when they see us (Genesis 26:28, 29; Malachi 3:12).

Has it ever occurred to you that God probably wants you to enjoy more prosperity than you have been enjoying? Once again I know what you are thinking. You're thinking, "I thought we are supposed to be content with what we have." We are, but what does that mean? To be content does not mean you can't have good things. It does not mean that you cannot have more than you have right now. I do not mean more to heap upon your lust, but more to glorify God. The devil has trained most of the Church to believe that less glorifies God, not more. The Bible does not teach that.

If less glorifies God, then Abraham, Isaac, Jacob, Joseph, King David, Solomon and Job did a lousy job of glorifying God, because God made them extremely rich. Our Heavenly Father did that in their lives, not the devil! If you will take time to read your Bible and check it out yourself, you will see that these men were not just spiritually rich, but abundantly financially and materially rich. According to Psalm 35:27, God has pleasure in the prosperity of His servant. Wow! These mighty men must have given God very great pleasure, don't you think? Wouldn't you like to do the same thing? Wouldn't you like to give your Father in Heaven great pleasure? I know I would!

The Apostle Paul said, "I know how to be abased, and I know how to abound..." (Philippians 4:11). He was not saying that God did not want him to have anything. In verse 18 of the same chapter he said, "Indeed I have all and abound. I am full..." He was teaching us what it means to be content. To be content means that things do not have us, but we have things. Idolatry is when we allow something or someone to come between us and God, when we allow something else to become first place in our lives. So the Lord was teaching us not to trust in riches but only in God. Maybe He wants you to live in a nicer home than you have considered living in. Maybe He wants you to drive a better car than you want to drive. Have you ever thought about that?

To be content means that I will go wherever God wants me to go and do whatever He wants me to do. If He wants me to go to a place where I will have to sleep in a hut or tent to get the Gospel to the people, then I will do it and rejoice in the Lord the whole time. If He wants me to live in a million-dollar home to get the Gospel to the people, then I will do that and rejoice in the Lord the whole time. My trust is in God, not man, money or things! I am content in Christ. Philippians 4:12 in one translation says I <u>know how to live independent of circumstances.</u> I believe the Apostle Paul was saying that no matter what is going on around me, opulence or poverty, I am going to maintain the joy of the Lord and trust my God to provide for me. I am not moved by circumstances! I am only moved by what I believe, and I believe God's Word! That is being content! Praise The Lord!

"Now godliness with contentment is great gain. And having food and clothing, with these we shall be content." (I Timothy 6:6, 8)

Some think these two verses are saying that loving the Lord and staying out of sin is all you need in this life. They try to make it sound as if that is the full definition of spirituality, and it's not! Once again they do not understand what it means to be content. If their explanation is correct then Adam, Eve, Abraham, Isaac, Jacob, Joseph, David, Solomon, Job and others were not content, because they didn't just have one cow to eat and one outfit to wear. They were the richest people on the face of the earth! And the devil didn't make them that way, God did! God's glory was manifested in their lives through their love for God, their walk of holiness and their wealth and riches (Haggai 2:7-9). But it was mainly through the blessings God bestowed upon them that the world recognized their God was the true God. Now I know that having wealth is not proof that a person is born again, but it is one of the blessings of being born again. Just because there are ungodly sinners experiencing financial prosperity does not mean God's children should not experience it. All of the gold, silver and good things on this earth were created by God for His people, not for the devil's bunch!

Obviously, this word contentment must be dealing with the motives of our hearts, and not so much as to what kind of car we drive. Why would God want abundant life, peace, joy, health and prosperity for His children? Because He loves us so much (just like you love your children), and because He wants to show the world how good He is to His children. Again, God wants to demonstrate to the world through His people that He is perfect love, all sufficient, our provider, healer, protector and that He put all the gold and silver in the earth and the cattle on a thousand hills for His family; not for the devil's family. Isaiah 61:9 in the Amplified Bible says:

"And their offspring shall be known among the nations and their descendants among the peoples. All who <u>see them [in their prosperity]</u> will recognize and acknowledge that they are the people whom the Lord has blessed."

One way to be a great witness for the Lord is to accept His prosperity in your life, while at the same time giving God great pleasure through blessing you. Let's look closer at Psalm 35:27.

"Let them shout for joy and be glad, who favor my righteous cause; and let them say continually, 'Let the Lord be magnified, who has pleasure in the prosperity of His servant.'"

God is not pleased for any of the curse of the law to operate in the lives of His children. If you truly want to please your Father in Heaven, then start developing your faith to walk in victory, wisdom, peace, holiness, perfect health and financial prosperity. Remember, we are not servants, we are sons and daughters of God (I John 3:1; Galatians 3:26; 4:6, 7). As sons and daughters we freely serve God, but we do not serve God because we are servants, but because we are sons who choose to serve. If God takes pleasure in the prosperity of His servants, how much more will He take pleasure in the prosperity of His sons. The Lord told us to shout for joy (not complain), and be glad (not sad), who favor His righteous cause. Favoring God's righteous cause is doing things God's way. Seeking His Kingdom first, trusting Him for everything, and always keeping Jesus as our first love; never allowing anything or anyone to come between us and the Lord. I Timothy 6:9, 17 say:

"But those who desire to be rich fall into temptation and a snare, and into many foolish and harmful lusts which drown men in destruction and perdition.

Command those who are rich in this present age not to be haughty, nor to trust in uncertain riches but in the living God, who gives us richly all things to enjoy."

The devil has lied to many in the Church by telling them that having money and material things would result in covetousness and lusting after things. Well, it is time we learn how to rightly divide the Word of God. Psalm 62:10 says:

"Do not trust in oppression, nor vainly hope in robbery; if riches increase, do not set your heart on them."

He did not say if riches increase you must get rid of them. He said do not set your heart on them. We are to set our hearts on God. Always seek Him first and obey His Word! Proverbs 11:28 says:

"He who trusts in riches will fall, but the righteous will flourish like foliage."

II Chronicles 26:5 said as long as King Uzziah sought the Lord, God made him prosper. So you see, God is not opposed to His people prospering because they are trusting Him as their provider, He is opposed to them trying to prosper without Him. Our Heavenly Father wants us to trust Him with all of our hearts and not to lean on our own understanding (Proverbs 3:5). Listen to me! You do not have to have money to be covetous. You can be flat broke and be covetous. You can be in debt up to your eye balls and burn with lust for material things. So, not having any money does not give you a deeper walk with the Lord, and it does not protect you from covetousness. The way to guard ourselves from covetousness is by maintaining a close walk with the Lord through constant prayer, staying full of His Word and obeying whatever the Holy Spirit tells us to do. Guess what? You can also be a multi-millionaire and walk in deep intimate fellowship with God. How would you do that? By trusting the Lord for everything and keeping Him first place in your life.

God is not opposed to His children being rich He's opposed to them being covetous. We have already looked at this some, but I want to say a few more words about it. If you noticed in I Timothy 6:17, God did not command those who are rich to get rid of their riches. He did not tell them that they would become covetous if they kept their riches. Also, He did not tell them that they could not be content with all of those riches did He? If contentment means you cannot have anything, then why didn't the Holy Spirit direct Paul to write that in the Bible? This verse would have been the perfect opportunity to tell all the rich people to get rid of their wealth, but if God had said that then He would have to repent for making Abraham, Isaac, Jacob, Joseph, David, Solomon, Job and others extremely rich.

What did He mean by saying that those who seek to be rich fall into temptation? He is speaking of those who seek to be rich because they want something else to trust in besides God. He is referring to people who are out to get rich, which is their goal in life. Their goal isn't to know God and spread His Word. Their goal is to accumulate as much money and things as they can. They do not have a heart for God or winning the lost to Jesus. They do not see anyone in life as important as they are. They are totally self-centered, instead of Jesus centered. I want to remind you of the story of a rich man who got caught in covetousness. Mark 10:17-22 says:

"Now as He was going out on the road, one came running, knelt before Him, and asked Him, 'Good Teacher, what shall I do that I may inherit eternal life?'

So Jesus said to him, 'Why do you call Me good? No one is good but One, that, God.

You know the commandments: 'Do not commit adultery,' 'Do not murder,' 'Do not steal,' 'Do not bear false witness,' 'Do not defraud,' 'Honor your father and your mother.'"

And he answered and said to Him, 'Teacher, all these things I have kept from my youth.'

Then Jesus, looking at him, loved him, and said to him, 'One thing you lack: Go your way, sell whatever you have and give to the poor, and you will have treasure in heaven; and come, take up the cross, and follow Me.'

But he was sad at this word, and went away sorrowful, for he had great possessions."

This man was operating in the old covenant and had obeyed the commandments of the Lord. I believe that is why he was rich, but instead of keeping God first in his life he allowed his possessions to come between him and the Lord. The Holy Spirit knew what was going on in the man's life and revealed it to Jesus. The

Bible says Jesus loved him. Jesus didn't tell him to sell everything and give to the poor because He was mad at him, and he did not tell him sell everything so he could be more spiritual. Obviously, God is the one who made him rich from obeying His commandments. At some point in this man's life he quit recognizing God as his first love, and began putting his trust in his possessions, but Jesus knew how to help him. There is nothing wrong with having material blessings, but there is something wrong when they have you.

Jesus response to the man was how God was able to shine the light on his covetousness. Jesus was not saying the answer to covetousness is selling everything, because you can be covetous and not have anything. I mentioned a few pages back that the way to guard ourselves from covetousness is to pray, stay full of God's Word and walk close with the Lord, but I want to share with you another very important protection from covetousness, and it comes from being a generous giver. Seedtime is a very effective means of counter acting covetousness. Think about this with me. What happens to Christians after they start prospering financially through their giving and then begin drifting over into covetousness? They start reducing their giving, and they start neglecting to bring in their tithes and offerings. Their possessions begin to take a stronger place in their lives than God, and they start holding on to more for themselves instead of giving more to bless others.

Jesus didn't tell the man to sell what he had so that he would not have anything anymore. He told him that after he sold his possessions he was to <u>give</u> to the poor; which meant to have seedtime. The Lord was simply telling the man that he needed to sow some seed. Well, if the man had remembered (and believed) what God said in Genesis 8:22, that harvest time accompanies seedtime, he would not have been sad by what Jesus told him. Yet, he was so blinded by his greed he did not recognize that Jesus was telling him how to keep God first in his life and become even richer than he was before. **Don't ever let your talent, gifts, abilities and prosperity take you to where your character can't keep you!!**

My goal in life is not to be rich! My goal and heart's desire is to know Jesus and the power of His resurrection! To please and glorify God in every area of my life! To win the lost to Jesus and make disciples of all the nations! To be the kind of testimony to the world that I am (in Christ) the blessed of the Lord, and I serve the true and only God! I pray that you will have the same goal. If you remember again I Timothy 6:17, it says that God (not the devil) is the one who gives us richly all things to **enjoy**. All things mean all things.

God wants us to be rich or prosperous in every area of our lives. III John 2 says:

"Beloved, I pray that you may <u>prosper in all things</u> and be in health, just as your soul prospers."

To be rich physically is to walk in perfect health. To be rich mentally is to have peace of mind and your mind renewed to God's Word. To be rich financially should be obvious. But God said He gives us richly all things to **enjoy.** Yes, He definitely gives us all things to enable us in spreading the Gospel throughout the earth, but He did not say that in I Timothy 6:17 did He? He's talking in this verse about actually enjoying your prosperity; experiencing great joy from His abundant blessings. Do you see how He tied His riches in with pleasure and enjoyment? Who's enjoyment? Yours! God wants you and your family to **enjoy** His goodness <u>and</u> to have plenty to give to every good work (II Corinthians 9:6-15)!

Let me sum up what I have been saying. First and foremost, we need to make sure we always give out of a heart of love (as we purpose in our hearts). Give your tithes and offerings as a way to express to the Lord how much you love Him and appreciate all He's done for you. Second, give to be a vessel for God to use in financing the Gospel into every nation. Third, give because you expect to reap a harvest. If you do not reap your harvest you will run out of seed to sow. You must release your faith and expect your harvest to come to you. God is the one who gives us the harvests, but we have to reap them. If your harvest is for money, expect money to come to you every day! Expect people to give good things, great financial blessings into your life everywhere you go; even as God works through you the same way in blessing others! Fourth, give so God can make you and your family a greater testimony to the world that you are the blessed of the Lord, then His glory on you will be seen by others and will draw the lost to where you are so they can get saved (Isaiah 60:1-5).

So let's get in agreement with God's perfect will for our lives!

The Prosperous Seed

CHAPTER
2

ACTIVATE THE BLESSING

It was in the very beginning that God created man to walk and live in His blessing.

"Then God said, 'Let Us make man in Our image, according to Our likeness; let them <u>have dominion</u> over the fish of the sea, over the birds of the air, and over the cattle, over all the earth and over every creeping thing that creeps on the earth.'

So God created man in His own image; in the image of God He created him; male and female He created them.

Then God blessed them, and God said to them, 'Be fruitful and multiply; fill the earth and subdue it; <u>have dominion</u> over the fish of the sea, over the birds of the air, and over every living thing that moves on the earth.'" (Genesis 1:26-28)

To be fruitful and multiply would of course mean to populate the earth, but it also means to succeed and prosper in all that you do. Plus, God told them to subdue the earth and have dominion. That sounds to me like God wanted them to rule and reign as kings in life, to eat the good of the land (Isaiah 1:19). But how were they going to do that? Verse 28 tells us how. It was through <u>the blessing</u>. God put a blessing on them, but what does that mean? I dare say most Christians do not know what the blessing means. The reason I say that is because of the way most people use the term "God bless you". A perfect example of this is when someone sneezes. What do they say? Bless you or God bless you. Now, if you will stop and think about that for a moment, you will realize how dumb it sounds to say God bless you when a person sneezes.

What does the phrase God bless you have to do with sneezing? How come you don't say that when someone burps, laughs or coughs? Who in the world came up with that anyway? Here is what has happened. Man has taken the phrase God bless you and turned it into a cutesy little saying. Do you know why? Because they do not have a clue as to what the blessing of the Lord actually means. Listen now. The blessing of the Lord is an empowerment. It is an enablement from God that He put on man so he could be fruitful and prosper. Deuteronomy 8:18 says:

"And you shall remember the Lord your God, for it is He who gives you <u>power to get wealth</u>, that He may establish His covenant which He swore to your fathers, as it is this day."

The power to get wealth is the blessing. The Lord did not say He gives us wealth, but He gives us the power or the enablement to get wealth. God did not tell Adam and Eve that He had already made them as fruitful and prosperous as they would ever be. The Bible says God blessed them and commanded them to be prosperous and take dominion. It was through the blessing, His enablement and empowerment upon them that they could get wealth and be fruitful. They had to learn how to operate in the blessing didn't they? Let me say it this way. They had to learn how to activate that blessing, and guess what? Sneezing will not activate it. Look with me at what Proverbs 10:22 says.

"The blessing of the Lord <u>makes</u> one rich, and He adds no sorrow with it."

If you notice in that verse, the blessing of the Lord <u>makes</u> one rich. That tells me that the blessing does something. First, the blessing is from the Lord. Second, the blessing is designed to <u>make</u> you rich not broke, and when you get rich through God's blessing you will experience joy not sorrow. Sorrow comes to the world when they try to get rich through their own efforts, without trusting God. But when you let the blessing of the Lord make you rich through your faith in God, He adds no sorrow with it. Joy, peace and victory always accompany God's blessing.

Now I know for many Christians, the word rich bothers them. They have been taught that the word rich is unspiritual and ungodly. They need to read the first chapter of this book. Maybe the Lord will lead you to buy an extra copy and bless them with it. They act like the word rich is a cuss word. I know it's a four letter word, but it is not a cuss word. Remember, God (your Heavenly Father) is the one who used that word in His Bible. The word rich (in Hebrew is ashar) means to accumulate, grow or make rich. God did that for Abraham in Genesis 13:2, "**Abram was very <u>rich</u> in livestock, in silver, and gold.**" Also, II Corinthians 8:9 says:

"For you know the grace of our Lord Jesus Christ, that though He was rich, yet for your sakes He became poor, that you through His poverty might become <u>rich</u>."

Just like salvation and healing are in the atonement (our redemption through the precious Blood of Jesus) so prosperity is also in the atonement. Whether you have been taught correctly or not, God has made **you** <u>very rich</u> in Christ, and I am not just talking spiritually. Abram's riches in livestock, silver and gold were not spiritual, but material and financial. Praise God! Abraham is considered our father of faith. We learn from his example. Part of the fruit from his spiritual walk with God was great prosperity, and today

28

God wants us to prosper financially and be in health even as we (or in direct proportion to) prosper spiritually (III John 2).

We are still talking about activating the blessing on our lives. The blessing of the Lord was not bestowed upon us to be passive. It has to be activated to enable us to prosper financially and in every area of our lives. I am bringing this point out because there are probably thousands of Christians who are not aware that the blessing on them needs to be activated.

Let me explain further. The Bible teaches that salvation and healing are for everyone (see our book "Healing is God's will for Everyone"), but even though that is true not everyone will receive and experience salvation and healing. There are Christians who will live their entire life with disease in their bodies, and then die and go to Heaven, and never experience the healing that belonged to them while on the earth. What does that mean? It means they never activated God's blessing on them for Divine healing. No matter what they were experiencing in their bodies, healing was still God's will for them. Healing was available for them to enjoy every day of their lives, but they never activated God's healing blessing.

The same is true for prosperity. If you stay broke all your life and can hardly make ends meet, don't blame God, it's not His fault. God finished everything for us in Christ at Calvary, but all of the wonderful blessings and benefits that are now ours (in His grace) will not automatically materialize in our lives just because we love the Lord. Every Believer is the blessed of the Lord. The blessing of Abraham is upon every Believer and we are also blessed with every spiritual blessing in the Heavenly places in Christ (Ephesians 1:3). Galatians 3:13, 14 tell us that Christ redeemed us from the curse of the law (sin, sickness and poverty) and <u>blessed us</u> with the blessing of Abraham. But, you and I can carry that blessing around all of our lives and never fully experience what it can do.

Once again, God gave us example after example through His men and women in the Bible of what His blessing can do. I do not believe that anyone has ever fully tapped into the greatness of God's blessing except for the Lord Jesus Christ. Why don't you and I make a commitment before God to allow Him to develop our faith stronger and stronger in walking in financial prosperity? Why don't we totally yield to the Holy Spirit so He can make us the biggest financial channels we can be for the work of God?

Let's go back to the beginning one more time. God revealed to us in Genesis chapter one, while describing the creation, the main way to activate the blessing, the main way to take dominion and to finance the Gospel throughout the world. Genesis 1:28 told us that God blessed man so he could be fruitful and prosper, <u>but then in verse 29 God</u> <u>showed us how to activate His blessing</u>.

"And God said, 'See, I have given you every herb that yields <u>seed</u> which is on the face of all the earth, and every tree whose fruit yields <u>seed</u>; to you it shall be for food.'"

The way to activate God's blessing and take dominion is through the **seed**! The way for you to get out of debt and to eat the good of the land is through the **seed**! The way for God to use you in expanding His Kingdom by taking the Gospel into every nation is through the **seed**! The way you are going to live independent of this world's economy is through the **seed**! It is through <u>seedtime and harvest</u>, that's the way God's Kingdom works.

God told Adam and Eve that every herb and tree would yield seed for them, why? He wanted them to have plenty of food. Did that require them to eat their seed? No, they were to use the seed for a harvest which would result in food for their family. Food represents sustenance and what Adam needed to support his family, or you could say to pay the bills. So again, what was the seed for? The seed was to sow for a harvest, or you could say that he was to **sow for a living**. He was to use his seed to sow for a living, and out of its harvests he would have more seed to sow, more food for his family, and more to bless others. This is God's Divine cycle for all Believers. Every harvest you and I reap is a demonstration of our victory and dominion over the devil and this world! The way to take dominion over sickness and financial lack is through the seed! The way to experience the victory that is already yours in Christ is through the seed! The way to enjoy rest and peace all of the time is through the seed! The way to partake of the boundless grace of God is through the seed! I am talking about seeds sown in faith out of your trust in God! So let's sow a lot of seed into God's Kingdom! We need to always be supernatural, Spirit led sowers and reapers. Genesis 8:20-22 says:

"Then Noah built an altar to the Lord, and took of every clean animal and of every clean bird, and offered burnt offerings on the altar.

And the Lord smelled a soothing aroma. Then the Lord said in His heart, 'I will never again curse the ground for man's sake, although the imagination of man's heart is evil from his youth; nor will I again destroy every living thing as I have done.

While the earth remains, <u>Seedtime and harvest</u>, cold and heat, winter and summer, and day and night <u>shall not cease</u>.'"

After the flood receded during Noah's adventure, he built an altar and offered sacrifice to the Lord. Then the Lord said that while the earth remains <u>seedtime and harvest</u> shall not cease. He also said in verse 22 that cold and heat, winter and summer, and day and night shall not cease. God listed some major events that take place on our planet continually. They always happen don't they? And they always will while the earth is here. If I told you the sun will not come up in the morning, you would not believe me would you? If someone locked you in a room without windows for forty-eight hours, then told you the sun never came up while you were in there, you would not believe him would you? Even though you could not see outside your room, you would stake your life on the fact that the sun still came up and went down while you were in there. You would be 100% confident of that fact wouldn't you?

Well guess what? God put the principle and law of seedtime and harvest in the same company with these other world events. What was He trying to tell us? God wants you and me to be just as confident that when we sow our seed we will reap our harvest as we are confident that the sun will come up in the morning and go down at night! Here is what this should mean to you. If someone told you that your harvest from the tithes and offerings you gave will not come to pass, you would have to call them a liar. They would not be able to dissuade you! They would not be able to shake your faith! You know just like you know the sun will come up tomorrow that your harvest <u>will be</u> <u>manifested</u>! And you expect your harvest to come to pass with as much confidence as you expect the Sun to come up in the morning! Galatians 6:7 says, **"Do not be deceived, God is not mocked; for whatever a man sows, that he will also reap."** He did not say that he might reap or it's a good chance he will reap. He said he <u>will</u> reap! God set it up to work this way in the very beginning and we are not going to change it. Now, let me insert a warning here. We also need to watch what we sow. Don't take sowing and reaping lightly.

"For he who sows to his flesh will of the flesh reap corruption, but he who sows to the Spirit will of the Spirit reap everlasting life.

And let us not grow weary while doing good, for in due season we shall reap if we do not lose heart.

Therefore, as we have opportunity, let us do good to all, especially to those who are of the household of faith." (Galatians 6:8,10)

The world does this all of the time and so do a lot of Christians. They just live any way they want to and do anything they want to do. They could care less what God thinks about it or even if it displeases Him. They think they're getting away with sin, but they are going to reap an awful harvest. If you sow to the flesh you will reap corruption! You can stick your head in the sand as much as you want, but your harvest is coming up! Ecclesiastes 10:8 says, **"He who digs a pit will fall into it, and whoever breaks through a wall will be bitten by a serpent."** The good news is God loves you and if you will repent to Him, and ask Him for His mercy and help, He will give it to you. He is good at turning our messes around to work out for our good and His glory.

Let me share with you why many of us (Christians) have not experienced the kind of financial harvest and breakthroughs we need to experience. If a Christian farmer came to you to agree with him in prayer for a big corn harvest this year, you would probably agree with him. After acknowledging that agreement, he then might tell you that he is standing in faith, pleading the Blood of Jesus, doing some fasting and has started a prayer chain of a 1000 other Christians for his harvest. Right at first you would probably think that he is really trying to put works with his faith, but when you ask him if he sowed any corn seed, he answers with a no. You then ask him why not?

In which case he responds, "My family and I had to eat our corn seed. We could not afford to plant it in the ground, but we still have our faith applied for God to bless us with a big corn harvest." Will that work? Will he get a corn harvest? Absolutely not!! Just because you did all the other good spiritual things does not excuse you from planting corn seed! Then the devil will lie to the farmer by feeding on his discouragement and telling him that faith does not work and God does not answer prayer. It should be very clear to us that it was not God's fault. It was the farmers fault for not sowing any seed. He wanted a harvest without having seedtime first.

Here is where many of us have missed it the same way. We have gone to a fellow Believer and asked him to agree with us in Jesus' Name that great financial blessings will come to us so we can pay our rent, house payment, car payment, and credit card debt and so on, but have not sown any financial seed. It's true; we were acting correctly by releasing our faith in prayer. Faith in God works and He answers prayer, but if we want a financial harvest we must sow financial seed. Even though we are obeying other great principles in the Bible, we cannot neglect seedtime and harvest! If someone asks us if we are a tither and giver, we would probably give him the same answer as that farmer. It would sound something like this, "We would love to tithe and give but we cannot afford it." Listen! You cannot afford not to tithe and give! Let me share with you something you should always remember. **You can sow your way out of debt**! But you do it by faith in God.

This is not some "Christian" get rich quick scheme. Once again, fasting, praying, going to church, reading your Bible and having a good confession do not take the place of tithes and offerings. God will not break His law of sowing and reaping to give you or me a financial harvest if we are too lazy and stingy to sow our seed! Also, He will not give us a financial harvest if we are afraid to trust Him, step out in faith and sow our seed. If you want a harvest of financial prosperity you have to sow financial seed.

Remember, Genesis 8:22 used the phrase seedtime <u>and</u> harvest. The Bible did not say seedtime <u>or</u> harvest. It is not a choice. You do not get to decide that you are only going to have harvest time, and forget about seedtime.   When the Word says seedtime <u>and</u> harvest, it is telling us that the only way we will have a harvest is if we have a seedtime <u>first</u>. Here is more good news. By using the word <u>and,</u> the Lord is guaranteeing us that if we have a seedtime we will always have a harvest time. If you believe God's Word then you will believe this, and if you really believe this you will not become cold and lethargic the next time they take up an offering at your church. You will be on fire and excited that you have another opportunity to give because you know it's another opportunity to reap a financial harvest! Watch how the Lord Jesus used His faith to feed over 5,000 people in John 6:5-13.

"Then Jesus lifted up His eyes, and seeing a great multitude coming toward Him, He said to Philip, 'Where shall we buy bread, that these may eat?'

But this He said to test him, for He Himself knew what He would do.

Philip answered Him, 'Two hundred denarii worth of bread is not sufficient for them, that every one of them may have a little.'

One of His disciples, Andrew, Simon Peter's brother, said to Him,

'There is a lad here who has five barley loaves and two small fish, but what are they among so many?'

Then Jesus said, 'Make the people sit down.' Now there was much grass in the place. So the men sat down, in number about five thousand.

And Jesus took the loaves, and when He had given thanks He distributed them to the disciples, and the disciples to those sitting down; and likewise of the fish, as much as they wanted.

So when they were filled, He said to His disciples, 'Gather up the fragments that remain, so that nothing is lost.'

Therefore, they gathered them up, and filled twelve baskets with the fragments of the five barley loaves which were left over by those who had eaten."

Jesus asked Philip where they would buy bread to feed the people, but the Bible says He was testing Philip. Jesus knew what He would do. He knew how to meet this great need, and it was by a seed. That is why you are reading this book, to gain knowledge and understanding about seedtime and harvest, about the operation of God's Kingdom economy. I find it very interesting the way God used Jesus in feeding these people. If anyone had a perfect relationship with God, it was Jesus. If anyone had perfect faith it was Jesus. If anyone was sinless and walked in perfect love it was Jesus, but He still needed a seed to mix with His perfect faith to meet their need. The Father always answered Jesus' prayers didn't He? Why didn't He just pray and ask the Father to somehow cause enough food to supernaturally materialize for all of the people? Why didn't He just speak the food into existence?

While Jesus was on this earth He operated according to the same Kingdom laws we operate by. Please do not get the idea that the only reason we have to sow seed is because our faith is not strong enough to believe God for a harvest. The Holy Spirit led Jesus to use that little boys lunch as seed, to set an example for you and me to follow. When God wanted a harvest of many sons and daughters what did He do? Did He just speak them into existence? No, he set an example for us. He gave His greatest seed of all, His Son, God's indescribable gift! The Lord Jesus also gave Himself as a Seed, so we could become new creations in Him.

Back in John 6:7, Philip said that 200 denarii worth of bread would not be enough to meet this great need. He did not have a revelation about the power of the seed. He was consumed with the great need they were facing. Many of God's people are so covered up with their needs they cannot see the value of sowing seed. **We must become more seed conscious than we are need conscious**. I know when the bills are piled up it seems difficult to do that, but we have to start working on it. We have to become more conscious of what God can do for us through His grace in giving and receiving than what the devil has tried to do against us. We must renew our minds (our thinking and believing) to the Word of God; by doing that we are renewing and enlightening our spirits and minds to God's will for our lives. Look at what the Word says in Ecclesiastes 11:1, 2.

"Cast your bread upon the waters, for you will find it after many days.
Give a serving to seven, and also to eight, for you do not know what evil will be on the earth."

I want you to notice that God's advice for dealing with bad times is the opposite of the world's advice. He said even though evil (famine, bad economy, etc.) may come on the earth, we need to start casting our bread all over the waters, don't just give to seven but also give to eight. To paraphrase it, He saying no matter how bad it gets in the world, we need to give more and more. Now, the world will tell us to get all we can, stock up all we can and don't give anything to anyone, keep it all for ourselves because we may need it. The world's advice comes from people who are very need conscious, people who do not have a revelation of sowing and reaping, and who do not trust God as their provider. Why would our Heavenly Father tell us to give more and more despite reports of poverty and famine in the world? The economy of God's Kingdom operates differently than the economy of the world. God wants you and me to build up our Heavenly account so we will always have plenty of harvests to reap and we will never lack! The way to do that is by faithfully and consistently sowing; no matter how circumstances appear around us. Ecclesiastes 11:4 says:

"He who observes the wind will not sow, and he who regards the clouds will not reap."

What we observe with our natural eyes should be irrelevant to our giving. The wind and clouds represent any earthly distractions the devil would try to use to discourage you and me from sowing and reaping. You could say it this way, he who observes the bills and creditors will not sow. Also, he who observes the economy and the bad reports on the news will not sow. Many times when Christians go to the doctor they will ask you to agree with them for a good report (meaning a good report from the doctor or from man), but we need to realize that we already have a good report. God's Word is our report and the best report! God's report (Isaiah 53:1) is always true whether the doctor's report agrees with it or not!! It is fine to hear what the doctor has to say, but don't base your faith on his report. Man's report is always subject to change, but God's report is eternal truth and you can stake your life on it!! An excellent example of being a faithful sower in the midst of a terrible economy was the story of Isaac in Genesis 26: 1-6, 12-14.

"There was a famine in the land, besides the first famine that was in the days of Abraham. And Isaac went to Abimelech king of the Philistines, in Gerar.

Then the Lord appeared to him and said: 'Do not go down to Egypt; live in the land of which I shall tell you.

Dwell in this land, and I will be with you and bless you; for to you and your descendants I give all these lands, and I will perform the oath which I swore to Abraham your father.

And I will make your descendants multiply as the stars of heaven; I will give to your descendants all these lands; and in your seed all the nations of the earth shall be blessed; because Abraham obeyed My voice and kept My charge, My commandments, My statutes, and My laws.'

Then I Isaac sowed in that land, and reaped in the same year a hundred-fold; and the Lord blessed him.

So Isaac dwelt in Gerar.

The man began to prosper, and continued prospering until he became very prosperous; for he had possessions of flocks and possessions of herds and a great number of servants. So the Philistines envied him."

I feel like I cannot read this story enough. It is so faith building and relevant to our lives today. I don't think anyone is facing an economy worse than what Isaac faced. He learned how to take dominion over the bad economy through his seed didn't he? Now listen, God specifically instructed him to stay in the land of famine. God did not say I need you to get out of this land so I can prosper you. I believe the Lord used Isaac as an example of how to live independent of the world's economy. God reminded him that the blessing of Abraham was upon him. It seems as if God was saying to him, I want to show you how great this blessing is on your life, and I want you to know that nothing and no one can stop it from working for you!

Please pay close attention to this. Even though the blessing of the Lord was on Isaac, he still had to activate it before he could begin prospering. How did he do that? He did it through the seed. He put God's law of sowing and reaping into motion. Now I know that sounds real easy to agree with if you don't have any financial problems, but what would you do if the economy totally crashed and you lost your job? Are you sure that you know how to trust God and live by faith like Isaac did? The Bible says that Isaac sowed in the land during a famine and he reaped a hundred-fold return while in that famine. That's awesome! You may be in a terrible financial situation right now, and you need to know that the devil wants to use your situation (as Ecclesiastes says "the wind") to discourage you from giving. Why would he do that? Is he that concerned about you getting your bills paid? No, a thousand times No! He knows that despite how hard it may be for you right now, if you start faithfully giving and giving and giving into God's work, God will start giving into your work and you will come out of that financial pit of debt you're stuck in. The devil knows you can sow your way out of debt into financial abundance, but he is hoping that you don't know that.

Now, if you do find out about it, the devil is hoping you will not act on it.

Isaac did not let the awful economy stop him from sowing, and it did not stop him from reaping either. Think about this for minute. He reaped a hundred-fold return in the middle of a famine! That means I can sow my way out of any famine! I can sow my way out of any amount of debt! The famine did not stop Isaac from sowing and it did not stop God from giving him a huge harvest! Isaac began to prosper and he kept on prospering! Through sowing the seed of his faith, which includes his material and financial seeds, he was able to experience total victory over the famine and rule as a king in life! Everyone else around him was being dominated by the famine, but he and his family were living every day as though the famine did not exist! Everything he did prospered so much; he became a great testimony to the goodness of God. Even King Abimelech said that we have <u>seen</u> that the Lord is with you, and you are now the blessed of the Lord (Genesis 26: 28, 29).

Make the time to meditate God's Word on sowing and reaping. This will allow the Holy Spirit to develop your faith stronger in your giving and receiving. Also, become a systematic giver in the work of the Lord, while at the same time expecting your harvest to come to pass. Bring your tithes into the store house (where you are spiritually fed), financially support other ministries which are promoting the Gospel and give to the poor. Command your money to come to you in Jesus' Name! Bind the devil out of your finances! Tell him to take his hands off your money! Tell the angels to go get your money and bring it to you (Psalm 103:20; Hebrews 1:14). The angels hearken to and obey the voice of God's Word in your mouth. Rejoice and praise God until your harvest is manifested!

CHAPTER
3

WHAT DO YOU HAVE?

I like what one minister said, "You're not broke, you have a seed!" Never forget that! Look with me now at II Kings 4:1-7.

"**A certain woman of the wives of the sons of the prophets cried out to Elisha, saying, 'Your servant my husband is dead, and you know that your servant feared the Lord, and the creditor is coming to take my two sons to be his slaves.'**

So Elisha said to her, 'What shall I do for you? Tell me, <u>what do you have in the house</u>?' And she said, 'Your maidservant has nothing in the house but a jar of oil.'

Then he said, 'Go, borrow vessels from everywhere, from all your neighbors-empty vessels; do not gather just a few,

And when you have come in, you shall shut the door behind you and your sons; then pour it into all those vessels, and set aside the full ones.'

So she went from him and shut the door behind her and her sons, who brought the vessels to her; and she poured it out.

Now it came to pass, when the vessels were full, that she said to her son, 'Bring me another vessel.' And he said to her, 'There is not another vessel.' So the oil ceased.

Then she came and told the man of God. And he said, 'Go, sell the oil and pay your debt; and you and your sons live on the rest.'

This widow woman must have been in great debt for the creditors to insist on taking her sons to be slaves. The Bible says that she cried out to Elisha about it, and because God is so good He sent a prophet to speak into her life. He can also send a prophet to speak into your life, and you know what? He has already done that in a lot of ways by sending you a pastor. Your pastor is supposed to be God's mouth piece to you. I know it is not always like that in every church, but it should be. Some pastors are not even called to be pastors, they treat the ministry simply as a job where they can get a pay check, or they are pastoring a church to have a financial base to support their traveling ministry; but, there are genuine pastors out there who are truly called by God as shepherds over His flock. They love the sheep that they have been entrusted with, and their hearts desire is to feed and train them in the ways of the Lord. If you believe that God led and directed you to your local church then you need to bless and support your pastor and the church with your prayers, attendance and finances. You should expect the Lord to speak and minister to you by His Spirit every time you go to church.

So, the Lord spoke to this widow woman through the prophet Elisha and she ended up experiencing great prosperity. First, Elisha asked her a couple of questions, but it was the second question I want you to pay close attention to. He asked her if she had anything in the house. Now remember, she was broke. She was so far in debt she was about to lose her sons, yet Elisha wanted to know if she had anything, why? Obviously, he was thinking about seedtime and harvest, but she was not thinking the same way. He knew that she needed to sow a seed, but what good would that do? What good would it do for her to give when she was so deep in debt? Well, isn't that the way many of us have thought when it comes to giving? Why was it so important for her to give? She needed to sow a seed because it would give her a harvest through which she could pay off her debt. If you are in debt, you need a financial harvest don't you? Let me say it a little plainer. You need some money don't you? You may need a lot of money. I learned a long time ago that if I tell the bill collectors I love the Lord and attend church faithfully, they still want their money.

God wants you to have your money! He wants you to have plenty for you, your family and His Kingdom! If you will start sowing (in faith) into God's Kingdom, showing the Lord (over and over again) that you will be a faithful steward with the money He gives you while expecting great harvest to come into your life, you can sow your way out of debt into financial abundance! What would you say if a farmer took you out to his barn and showed you that it was full of all kinds of vegetables? Would you ask him how his barn became so full? I think you would. If his answer was "I sowed my way there" would that make sense to you? I believe it would. Why? You would understand that he sowed enough seed to reap enough harvest to fill up his barn.

Now, let's use the same example for our finances. What if you are financially debt free, your bank account is full and you are giving generously into God's Kingdom, and I ask you how you got that way. If you said "I sowed myself there", wouldn't it mean the same thing? God wants to use us (through faith and freely from His grace) in sowing our way out of debt into financial abundance! It is up to you and me to sow our seed and to reap our harvest. God does not reap the harvest for us. He gives us the harvest (He is the Lord of the harvest), but we must put the sickle in and reap it (Mark 4:26-29).

This widow woman could have sold what little oil she had and paid a fraction on her debt, but that would not have changed her financial situation enough to amount to anything. Actually that would do as little good in meeting her financial need as it would for her to simply eat her seed. Don't eat your seed!! If she did that, she would not have any seed to sow, she would not have a harvest or financial miracle coming her way and she would still be broke. So she made a wise decision. She chose to give what she had to the Lord by obeying God's instructions through the prophet. Those instructions were God's way of telling her how to reap her harvest. Her sons went out and gathered up vessels and when they came into the house they <u>shut the door behind them</u>. Why did they do that? They shut the door as if to say we are shutting the world out, we are shutting our unbelieving relatives out and we are shutting out all doubt and unbelief.

When you decide you are going to sow your way out of debt and become a financial channel for God's Kingdom expansion, there will be those who do not like that. There will be friends and family members who will think you are crazy. You will have to shut them out so to speak. Of course you have to walk in love towards them and may still have to talk to them, but at the same time, you don't have to believe and receive their words of fear and doubt. The way we spiritually guard ourselves from deception, fear and unbelief is by staying full of God's Word (Joshua 1:8). We do not have to hide in a monastery on a mountain in Tibet. Physically hiding out somewhere does not spiritually protect us. Remember the great commission? We are supposed to be leading the lost to Jesus. You cannot lead people to the Lord if you are never around them. We can always keep our spiritual guard of protection up everywhere we go by abiding in God's Word. By spending time in God's Word every day we are doing what Dr. Lester Sumrall used to say, "Feeding our faith and starving our doubts to death."

The Bible says that when the widow woman had filled up all of the vessels then the oil ceased. That tells me as long as she had vessels the oil would continue to flow. The oil did not stop flowing until she ran out of vessels. So don't run out of vessels! In other words, never stop and never slowdown in your giving! The oil flowing was her harvest wasn't it? I like to think of it this way. As long as you keep sowing your seed into God's Kingdom, the oil of your harvest will keep flowing. If you keep tithing and giving, you can expect to keep reaping financial harvest. It will never stop! Why? You already know why. God said as long as the earth remains seedtime and harvest <u>shall not cease</u>. The Lord guaranteed us that we can always expect to reap a harvest, or we can always expect the oil (which also represents God's anointing for breakthrough) to flow in our lives as long as we continue to have seedtime! So we are not only talking about financial harvest, but harvests or breakthroughs in every area of our lives.

You are the one who determines how much dominion, victory and blessings you will walk in on this earth. It will be in direct proportion to the harvests that you reap, and those harvests will be in direct proportion to the kind of seed you sow and the amount of seed you sow. Remember, Elisha asked the widow woman what she had. She said that she had nothing in the house but a jar of oil. Did you hear that? She said she had nothing, even though she had something. Because her need was so great, she believed that the little amount of oil she had was nothing compared to it; she did not realize she had a seed. When you have a seed you do not have "nothing"! She was more need conscious than she was seed conscious. We need to turn that around don't we? When you have a seed and will sow it, then you have all you need.

One reason many Christians do not get excited about giving into the work of the Lord is they do not understand the value of a seed. They do not have a reality of seedtime and harvest. When they compare their seed to their need, their seed looks puny. But if they understand the power of a seed and the harvest within it, they would not be afraid or worried about anything. If they would compare the harvest in their seed to their need, then their need would look puny. If you really saw the harvest in your seed, you would be full of joy and almost in a hurry to get your seed in the ground. Think about what Jesus did. Hebrews 12:2 says:

"Looking unto Jesus, the author and finisher of our faith, <u>who for the joy that was set before Him endured the cross</u>, despising the shame, and has sat down at the right hand of the throne of God."

This verse tells us how Jesus was able to endure the cross and all that He suffered. It was because of the joy that was set before Him. What does that mean? What Joy was set before Him? The joy He had when He thought about the harvest He and His Father would experience from the Seed of His death and resurrection. The Lord Jesus gave us the perfect example of how to look past your seed, that is, how to look inside your seed and see the harvest. He kept His mind on the harvest. He was able to endure all of the pain and suffering, and stay full of joy because He trusted the Father and kept His eyes on the harvest of many sons and daughters coming into the Kingdom! When you and I get a hold of this and really believe it, we will look forward to sowing. When the widow woman said she had nothing but a jar of oil, it was the same as saying I don't have anything but a seed. She did not know what she had and what it could do. Here is something else to remember, oil in the Bible represents the anointing of the Holy Spirit. In one sense, she was also saying I don't have anything but God's anointing. Wow! Think about that. In both cases she had more than enough and did not realize it. I hope you understand that you have a lot more than you think you do when you have a seed. Don't ever underestimate the power of a seed! Listen to what the Lord said in Mark 4:30-32.

"To what shall we liken the kingdom of God? Or with what parable shall we picture it?

It is like a mustard seed which, when it is sown on the ground, is <u>smaller than all the seeds</u> on earth;

But when it is sown, it grows up and <u>becomes greater than all</u> <u>herbs</u>, and shoots out large branches, so that the birds of the air may nest under its shade."

You may be planting the smallest of all seeds, but once it is sown, it grows up and becomes greater than all herbs. Did you catch that? A seed will not grow up until it is sown. I know that a three-year-old can understand that, but why can't adults? Why can't Christian adults understand that as long as all their money stays in their wallet and purse, they will not have a financial harvest? The seed must be sown! When you give your tithes and offerings into God's

Kingdom (where the Holy Spirit leads you to give), your seed becomes <u>a prosperous seed</u>.

"For <u>the seed shall be prosperous</u>, the vine shall give its fruit, the ground shall give her increase, and the heavens shall give their dew - I will cause the remnant of this people to possess all these." (Zechariah 8:12)

God was talking about the house of Judah and Israel here, but we can gain valuable insight from this for our lives today. The Lord Jesus was and is a very prosperous Seed, isn't He? Our Father God is still reaping sons and daughters into His Kingdom every day. So, what is a prosperous seed? I believe it's a seed sown in good ground which produces a bountiful harvest! It produces great fruit, increase and the blessings of Heaven being poured out on the sower! I like to confess, "My seed is prosperous in Jesus' Name! My seed always produces a great harvest for me!" Let me insert this declaration right here. As important as the seed is, it's still not my source. God is my provider, my only source for everything, He always supplies me with seed to sow and the harvest from my seed, and it comes freely from His grace through faith in Jesus' precious Blood. I in turn dedicate and commit all that I have to Him to be used totally for His praise and honor. Again, we are simply earthen vessels that the excellence of His glory and power flow through (II Corinthians 4:7).

The Prosperous Seed

CHAPTER
4

WORKING FOR A GIVING AND SOWING FOR A LIVING

Whenever you meet someone for the first time, you normally inquire as to what kind of work he does. The standard phrase is, "What do you do to earn a living?" It seems that every one says it the same way when referring to his or her job. The person usually says, "I do this type of work to <u>earn a living</u>." As Christians, when it comes to finances, our minds need to be greatly renewed to the Word of God. We need to quit thinking and talking the way the world does.

The Bible teaches that we are to receive everything we need and desire by faith and freely from God's grace. We could not earn anything from the Lord, but Jesus earned it all for us at Calvary. I would assume that the majority of Christians know that a person cannot earn his salvation. It is a free gift from God's grace. Many Christians also know that a person cannot earn his healing, deliverance, joy or peace. Those are free gifts from God's grace. So let me ask you a question. Why do you think you can earn a living? Now, you may be the type person who would quickly remind me that you cannot earn anything from God, but then turn right around and talk about how you earn a living or how you earn your money. If you really understand what Jesus did for us at Calvary, then you know that He redeemed us from the curse of the law (Galatians 3:13, 14). The curse included sin, spiritual death, sickness and <u>poverty.</u> In the place of the curse, He gave us righteousness, eternal life, health and prosperity (II Corinthians 8:9).

All of these gifts and blessings are free; we cannot earn any of them. The problem is, the devil and the world have trained most Christians to still think they are earning their money through their jobs. This is where we have to get our minds renewed to the Word. Remember, God gave you your job and He prospers you financially through it. If you think you are earning a living, then you are looking to yourself and your job as your source. Neither one is your source. God will supply all of your need (Philippians 4:19). The people of this world are humanistic; they don't think that they need anyone but themselves. They trust themselves. They trust their own abilities, and they do not believe that God gave them those abilities. They think that within themselves they are a "god". As the old saying goes, you cannot pull yourself up by your own boot straps.

We do not operate according to this world's financial system. We live in the Kingdom of God, and His Kingdom is also within us. We have been delivered out of the kingdom of darkness and translated into the Kingdom of light. We are living in this world but we are not part of it. I like to think about it this way. Even if we are physically standing about two feet from a lost person, spiritually speaking we are as far apart from each other as the east is from the west. We are living in two different kingdoms while on the same planet, and both kingdoms function by a different financial system. The world teaches people to accumulate and get all the money they can, and to never give any of it into the work of Lord. God's Kingdom teaches us to be generous and bountiful givers, and that the more we give away, the more we will get back. Now the world thinks that's crazy, they do not understand the ways of the Lord.

The Bible also says if you do not work, neither should you eat (II Thessalonians 3:10). Let me show you why we are to work.

"Let him who stole steal no longer, but rather let him labor, working with his hands what is good, that he may have <u>something to give</u> him who has need." (Ephesians 4:28)

This verse clearly tells us that the reason we work or labor is to have something to <u>give</u>, or to have seed to <u>sow</u>. So we need to change our thinking and our speaking. Begin confessing, "I am working for a giving." God is supplying us with seed to sow through all of our laboring. I know we need to use our money to pay bills, but we still need to become more seed conscious than bill conscious, more seed conscious than need conscious. When we get a revelation of seedtime and harvest, we will become more excited about going to work every day. Now here is the way we need to adjust our thinking and believing. Since we are not working to earn a living, then what are we doing? **<u>We are working for a giving and sowing for a living</u>**. We live and operate in God's Kingdom through sowing and reaping. Genesis 1:29 says:

"And God said, 'See, I have given you every herb that yields <u>seed</u> which is on the face of the earth, and every tree whose fruit yields <u>seed</u>; to you it shall be <u>for food</u>.'"

Let me repeat something from a previous chapter. God said the seed is for food. Food represents sustenance, and what we live by. Since God gives us seed for food, then He gives us seed to live by. Does that mean we are to eat our seed? No. We understand that the earth and God's Kingdom work by seedtime and harvest. The way we are to use our seed for food is to sow it, then live by the harvests. It is through our harvests that we have plenty of food for sustenance, as well as more seed to sow. Therefore, what is actually happening here? We are sowing for a living. Do you see it? Remember when Joseph was raised up as a great leader in Egypt? His relatives did not have any food. Really, they did not have any seed to plant to produce a harvest for food. They came to their brother Joseph and said:

"Why should we die before your eyes, both we and our land? Buy us and our land for bread, and we and our land will be servants of Pharaoh; <u>give us seed</u>, <u>that we may live</u> and not die, that the land may not be desolate." (Genesis 47:19)

To paraphrase it, they were saying, "Joseph, we sow for a living but we do not have any seed." Are you listening? What they needed was seed. I hope you are getting a hold of the fact that we work for a giving and we sow for a living. Many Christians are eating their seed. It is time we quit eating all of our seed! Start sowing more and you can expect to reap more. You may be a $5.00 giver right now, and that is fine, every seed is important (no matter how small), but don't be content to remain at that level of giving. You can start there but expect to increase. We must use our faith for finances like we do for everything else. Set goals in sowing and in reaping. <u>If you want to go to higher</u>

levels of receiving, you must go to higher levels of giving.

For example, you might decide to become a $20.00 giver, not that you can't give more, but you might want to start off by considering that your minimum amount when you give, but if you don't like that amount then pick the one you are comfortable with. Here is where faith comes in. You have to trust God and step out and give $20.00 when you are used to giving $5.00, then expect to reap a bigger harvest than you would from the $5.00 seed. Remember, this is not something that you try doing 3 or 4 times, but it is something that you continue doing until the greater harvests come in. Of course when greater harvests come in, then you can increase your level of sowing, maybe to $50.00 at a time. We need to start thinking this way. If we will not get discouraged and will make up our minds to live this way, then this cycle of sowing and reaping will get bigger and bigger. We will keep sowing more and reaping more.

God can bless you with harvests of raises and promotions on your job, but He can also cause money to come to you through other avenues. You might have a job that pays $2,000.00 a month, but through your prosperous seed God can cause another $3,000.00 to come in to you over and above your paycheck each month. There is no limit to what God can do in your finances through giving and receiving! You have to get a hold of this! You have to get a revelation of this! Even though you have known about the sowing and reaping Scriptures since you were a child, if you are still broke and financially struggling, that's proof that the power and importance of giving and receiving is not <u>real</u> to you yet. What do I mean by "real"? I mean that it needs to become rhema (God speaking it into your spirit - John 6:63) to you. Like a light coming on in your inner man, to where you will say, "I see it now! This is how I show God that I trust Him as my provider! And this is how I put myself in a place to receive what Jesus obtained for me at Calvary. My Father God works through my sowing and reaping to bring His blessings to pass in my life, and to supply my need according to His riches in glory by Christ Jesus." Remember, through God's grace He has already given me everything I will ever need and desire, but I still must appropriate it by faith. One of the main ways I release my faith for financial appropriation is through sowing and reaping.

Let me share with you how I think, and see if you think the same way to. If I am at church and the pastor makes an announcement that we need to expand our sanctuary, then my first thought will probably be on how God can use me in being a part of that. Many times pastors will tell their congregations about a church expansion by following it up with an announcement of all the special offerings they will receive for the next 2 or 3 years. I believe that we, as God's children and His heirs, should be able to stand up and say, "Pastor, you will not need to take up any offerings for that, I will write you a check for it at the end of the service." Wouldn't you like to be able to do that? Well how do we get to the place financially where we can? Here is how. We sow our way there in Jesus' Name! But we will never get to that place if we do not start where we are right now and with the money we have right now. If we will not give God one dollar from the ten dollars He gave us, then we will not give Him one hundred thousand dollars as the tithe from a million dollars.

Once again, to receive on a higher level, we have to give on a higher level. To reap more financially we have to sow more financially. Like I said, we have to sow our way there. We have to show our Father God that we will pass His tests and be faithful stewards with the money He gives us. We need to show the Lord that we will never allow increase in prosperity to cause us to slow down in our pursuit of more intimate fellowship with Him. We also need to show the Lord that no matter how much He blesses us, we will stay faithful in living a holy life, going to church and serving Him with all our hearts. If God gives us a new boat, we will not skip church on Sundays to go out to the lake. If we will always seek God and His righteousness (His way of living) first, then everything else we need and desire will be added unto us (Matthew 6:33). If we don't want to go on this financial adventure, we don't have to. We can scrape by all our lives and never be the kind of financial channels God desires of us. But I hope that is not the way you think and believe. I hope that you are like Leia and me. I hope that your heart's desire is to know Jesus and the power of His resurrection and to do great exploits in His Name (Daniel 11:32)! I expect to do great exploits in winning the lost to Jesus, to be used by the Lord in doing great exploits in healings and miracles for the people and also in doing great exploits financially through sowing and reaping! Can you agree with that for your life?

The Prosperous Seed

CHAPTER 5

CAN YOU BELIEVE GOD FOR THE HUNDRED-FOLD RETURN?

The hundred-fold return harvest was one of the first financial miracles that I ever experienced. God did that for me before someone told me that you cannot expect the Lord to do that for you. I am so glad I have never listened to people like that. I decided to listen to the Bible and just do what it says. God said it and that settles it! I believe it and that settles it for me! So, let me show you from the Scriptures where God has settled it.

"Then Peter began to say to Him, 'See, we have left all and followed You.'
So Jesus answered and said, 'Assuredly, I say to you, there is no one who has left house or brothers or sisters or father or mother or wife or children or lands, for My sake and the gospel's, who shall not receive a hundred-fold now in this time-houses and brothers and sisters and mothers and children and

lands, with persecutions-and in the world to come, eternal life.

But many who are first will be last, and the last first.'" (Mark 10:28-31)

It was the Lord Jesus who said this about the hundred-fold. He used the term hundred-fold didn't He? He not only talked about the hundred-fold but said it was for <u>now in this time.</u> He did not say anything about waiting to get to Heaven to experience the hundred-fold return. Now in this time means right now on this earth. You do not have to study Greek or Hebrew to understand that. You do not need a theologian to explain it either. So what do we need to understand from these verses? It is very important to listen to what Peter said before you hear what Jesus said. Peter said <u>we have left all and followed You</u>. It sounds to me like Jesus was responding to what Peter said. It also sounds to me like Jesus was describing the harvests that Peter could expect from his seed. You may ask what seed? It was the seed of his life. Peter sowed the biggest seed he could sow didn't he? He first gave his life to the Lord. He sowed his life as a seed into God's work. It was after that commitment and dedication that Jesus said there is no one who has left...or given into God's Kingdom who shall not receive a hundred-fold now in this time.

Does this have to do with finances and material things? Of course it does. To leave houses and lands refers to giving them up or sowing them into the work of the Lord. Houses and lands represent money, cars, clothes, houses, lands, airplanes and etc. Please listen closely to what I am about to say! The hundred-fold return isn't like a Christian rabbit's foot. God was not saying that you can live in sin, skip church and maybe serve Him about ten percent of the time and then give Him ten dollars and He will give you back one thousand. To paraphrase it, Peter said we have left all. We have totally dedicated our lives to serving you and doing your will, so now what happens to us? Then Jesus said to Peter whatever you sow into my Kingdom, you can expect to receive a hundred-fold return. Receiving or reaping harvests takes faith, just like it takes faith to sow our seed. The hundred-fold is not God's limit on how much He can bless us. God knows no limit. He is just giving us an example of what we can believe Him for. You may not want to start believing God for a hundred-fold return. You may want to start with tenfold or thirtyfold. We grow into this. We need to develop our faith in sowing and reaping by sowing more and in reaping more. In Matthew 13:23, Jesus was telling the parable about four different people who heard the Word, but only the fourth person produced a harvest.

"But he who received seed on the good ground is he who hears the word and understands it, who indeed bears fruit and produces: some a <u>hundred-fold</u>, some <u>sixty</u>, some <u>thirty</u>."

Here the Lord talks about a hundred-fold, sixtyfold and thirtyfold return harvest. You may not get a hundred-fold return on everything, but like Jesus said according to your faith be it unto you. Why would the Lord tell us this if it was not obtainable? Of course the hundred-fold return harvest is also spiritual fruit produced in our lives: spiritual growth, love, joy, peace, etc. But still, the Lord made it very clear that we can expect to receive houses and lands, which represent financial and material prosperity. Remember what happened to Isaac in Genesis 26:12? The emphasis is on the hundred-fold return in financial and material blessings.

"Then Isaac sowed in that land, and reaped in the same year a <u>hundred-fold</u>; and the Lord blessed him."

If you read the preceding verses you will see that Isaac was in a land of famine, yet he still sowed or you could say he still gave his tithes and offerings. He did not allow the economy or circumstances to stop him from sowing (now that takes faith-trust in God as your provider), and he reaped a hundred-fold return in the middle of a famine. If God would do that for Isaac (a man that wasn't born again or in the new covenant which we are part of) He will do it for you in your situation. God is no respecter of persons. The Lord would not give Isaac a hundred-fold return on his seed and not you. Let me give you another Scripture that talks about the hundred-fold.

"You will chase your enemies, and they shall fall by the sword before you.
Five of you shall chase a hundred, and a hundred of you shall put ten thousand to flight; your enemies shall fall by the sword before you."
(Leviticus 26:7, 8)

Five people chasing away a hundred would be considered a twenty-fold return wouldn't it? Hundred people putting ten thousand to flight would be a hundred-fold return victory. This was not referring to a spiritual hundred-fold return; it was a hundred-fold return of victory in the natural realm. Deuteronomy 1:11 even speaks of a thousand-fold return. I just wanted to share that with you to spark your thinking. Please also remember that the fruit or harvest from the seed we sow will be according to its kind. Genesis 1:12 says:

"And the earth brought forth grass, the herb that yields seed according to its kind, and the tree

that yields fruit, <u>whose seed is in itself according to its kind</u>. And God saw that it was good."

If the Lord uses you in sowing love, joy and peace into others, then expect to reap a hundred-fold return of love, joy and peace. I am not sure how you can accurately measure that, or even if you need to try, but God said our harvest or fruit will be based on the type or kind of seed that we sow. Therefore, it makes sense that if you sow financial seed you should reap a financial harvest. One thing about financial and material harvests, they can be measured. If the hundred-fold return is only for a "spiritual" harvest, then how could you measure that? Why would Jesus (in Matthew 13:23 and Mark 10:29, 30) give us specific numbers identifying levels of harvest if He did not want us to believe Him for specific amounts. I just don't see Jesus saying, "You can reap 30, 60 and 100 fold harvests, but you will never know when you do."

Again, in Mark 10:29, 30, Jesus identified specific and detailed hundred-fold return harvests that can be measured and that we can experience, right now in this time! No matter how difficult it may be for us to wrap our heads around these two verses, Jesus still said it, His Word is true, and He made it very clear that it is for our lives here and now. I am sure there is much more revelation we have not yet seen from these Scriptures, so let's be open to whatever the Holy Spirit wants to show us. The Bible clearly teaches the hundred-fold return principle, but that does not mean that every time you give you must expect a hundred-fold return on it. You have a free will, you can decide what you want to use your faith for, and that will be determined upon the development of your faith. The Word says he who sows bountifully will reap bountifully, and that is true in every realm, which includes the financial realm. Therefore, we can always expect to reap more than we sowed. Well, how much more? Did God give us any kind of an idea on what levels of returns we could expect to receive? He sure did. I hope that you have received more light on this great subject. It might help to refresh your memory by reading again the Scriptures in this chapter.

As I mentioned at the beginning of this chapter, I want to share with you one of the first financial miracles I received from the Lord. God made the hundred-fold return principle real to me when I was twenty years old while attending Christ For The Nations Bible Institute in Dallas, Texas. I had never heard of believing God for a hundred-fold harvest, until I received a ministry magazine with teaching on that very subject. While at Bible school I was also on the radio Monday through Friday teaching the Word of God. One day I contacted the manager at the radio station and he said that I owed him $280.00 for radio time.

Well at that time I was a Bible school student and I was broke. Two hundred eighty dollars to me at that time was like ten thousand dollars. I did not have either one. But after reading Mark 10: 28-30 in this ministry magazine, I got inspired. Faith cometh by hearing doesn't it? I got my Bible out and opened it to Mark, chapter ten, and spent some time meditating on those verses. I then got out my check book to see if I had any money in it. I had enough to write a check for $3.00. I decided that I would sow it as seed in the next Sunday morning offering. (I am so glad no one told me that you cannot believe God for a hundred-fold return, because I just decided to believe what Jesus said.) I prayed over my seed and claimed a hundred-fold return of $300.00 from my $3.00 seed in Jesus' Name! For the next two and a half weeks, whenever I thought about it, I would praise and thank the Lord for my hundred-fold return of $300.00.

Now listen, I did not tell anyone about this. I did not try to help God by hinting to people that I needed some money. I expected a supernatural miracle to come to pass. Only the Lord and I knew about the seed I sowed. So, about two and a half weeks later I sat down to eat lunch in the school cafeteria and another student sat down at the table across from me. Personally I did not know the young man sitting in front of me, and I did not know that he knew I was on radio. I think God likes to bless us, many times, through people and ways that we least expect. While I was eating, the man asked me a question. He said how is your radio ministry doing? I could have given him a sob story and told him how desperate I was for some money, but I didn't. I decided to stay in faith and trust God as my source. I said to him, "The radio ministry is doing great in Jesus' Name!" He said, "I thought I might help you out if that is ok?" I said, "That would be great." Then he said, "Would $300.00 help you?" I tried not to act real excited and calmly said, "Yes it would."

Let me ask you this, out of all the numbers he could have chosen why did he choose the number 300? I will tell you why, that was exactly 100 times what I gave God two and a half weeks ago. He then asked me to come up to his room to give me a check. I know it was not a lot of money, but it was 100% supernatural from God. I remember standing there holding that $300.00 check in my hand and thinking about the $3.00 check I gave to God in the offering. Yes, I do believe in the hundred-fold return!

Another time I was in a service when the offering was being received, I wanted to give but I was not sure if I had any cash on me. I looked in my wallet and took out a $5.00 bill and sowed in the offering. I prayed over it, asked the Lord to use it in blessing His work through that church and I claimed a hundred-fold return of

$500.00 in Jesus' Name! As soon as the service was over and I had stepped out of the main sanctuary into the foyer area, the pastor of the church approached me. He thanked me for coming to the service and said that he wanted to bless me with a check. Can you guess how much it was for? You're right, $500.00! Let me be honest with you. I cannot say that I have seen that happen every time I have given. The Bible does not guarantee that you will never reap less than a hundred-fold return on your seed. You may reap a 5 fold, 12 fold, 23 fold, 35 fold, 50 fold, etc. It depends on what kind of seed you sow, what kind of soil you sow it into and what you believe God for.

In Luke 6:38, Jesus told us that when we give, we can expect a harvest to be given unto us good measure, pressed down, shaken together and running over. That sounds like He was describing different amounts of harvests (or different folds) coming back to us. When the Lord said to give, He was referring to giving forgiveness, love, your time, money and many different kinds of seed wasn't He? It sounds to me like we should always expect our harvests to be greater than the seed we sow, but that doesn't mean it will always be a hundred-fold or greater. Still, let's not forget that Jesus did say all things are possible to him who believes (Mark 9:23)! He also told us that the hundred-fold return is for now in this time, and He included within it houses and lands. So, I keep stretching my faith to believe God to sow more and to reap more. We all should be constantly increasing in our giving and receiving.

Let's become more conscious in using our faith for what we sow and for what we reap. Let's practice believing God for greater specific amounts to give and for greater specific amounts to receive. How will you know if you got a 30, 60 or 100 fold return back from the Lord if you don't even know how much you gave or how much the hundred-fold return would be? Maybe you should start paying more attention to what you sow and what you reap. Faith works the same in every realm, our finances are not excluded. I want to be the biggest giver I can be in God's Church, don't you? If I want to go from bench pressing 100 lbs to bench pressing 300 lbs that would take a good deal of time wouldn't it? I would have to do a lot of exercising wouldn't I? Well it works the same way with our faith. It takes a lot of time and practice. The key is to always keep sowing, keep stretching your faith expecting to sow more and to reap more. Be vigilant about it! Don't let the devil or the economy talk you out of it! All your money as well as all the blessings of Heaven belong to you, so don't let the devil have them! Don't let the devil steal from you what God has freely given you in Christ! You can take dominion over the devil and rule and reign in life through the seed, but first, you have to sow it, and after you sow it, <u>it becomes a prosperous</u> <u>seed</u>!

CHAPTER
6

IMPORTANT REVELATION ABOUT THE TITHE

In case you picked up this book, skipped over to this chapter to find out what I will say about tithing to determine if you will even read this book, then let me go ahead and settle it for you right now. I believe that tithing is very important, it is part of our new covenant and every Christian should joyfully give their tithes and offerings into God's Kingdom. Now, if you believe that, you will definitely want to read this chapter. If you do not believe that then you will definitely want to read this chapter. I have been teaching on tithing for over three decades and the Lord has opened my spiritual eyes to some things I had never seen before. As a result, I am experiencing a greater faith, excitement and freedom in tithing. I want to tithe and give more than ever, but not because I have to, not because I am commanded to and not because a curse may come on me if I don't. So, let's start off by looking at some verses in Hebrews 7:1-9.

"For this Melchizedek, king of Salem, priest of the Most High God, who met Abraham returning from the slaughter of the kings and blessed him,

To whom also Abraham <u>gave a tenth</u> part of all, first being translated "king of righteousness," and then also king of Salem, meaning "king of peace,"

Without father, without mother, without genealogy, having neither beginning of days nor end of life, but made like the Son of God, remains a priest continually.

Now consider how great this man was, to whom even the patriarch Abraham <u>gave a tenth</u> of the spoils.

And indeed those who are of the sons of Levi, who receive the priesthood, have a commandment to receive tithes from the people according to the law, that is, from their brethren, though they have come from the loins of Abraham;

But he whose genealogy is not derived from them received tithes from Abraham and blessed him who had the promises.

Now beyond all contradiction the lesser is blessed by the better.

Here mortal men receive tithes, but there he receives them, of whom it is witnessed that he lives.

Even Levi, who receives tithes, <u>paid tithes</u> through Abraham, so to speak."

If you remember the story, God gave Abraham a great victory in battle, and then he met a man named Melchizedek to whom he gave a tithe. Melchizedek was a priest of the Most High God, therefore he represented God. So you could say Abraham tithed to God through this man. Abraham lived in the old covenant and he gave this tithe to Melchizedek about 450 years before the law was given to Israel through Moses. Also in Genesis 28:22, Jacob made a vow to God that he would give Him a tenth or tithe of all God blessed him with. So you can see that tithing was definitely before the law was given. I realize you probably know this, but I need to lay a little bit of a foundation about the tithe first. Now the main Scriptures we usually read about tithing are in Malachi. The teaching about tithing in Malachi was when the nation of Israel was under the law. Then we have tithing revealed in the new covenant in verse 8 of this chapter we just read in Hebrews. Tithing did not start with the law. Tithing was before the law, during the law and after the law. There were some things that were different though about tithing during the law compared to tithing now under grace in the new covenant, and we are going to look at some of those things.

Hebrews 7:8 says here mortal men receive tithes. I want to mention again that the Hebrew word for tithe means a tenth, but it also means to accumulate. In the mind of unbelievers and maybe a lot of Christians that may sound contradictory, but that is how God's Kingdom economy works. God says when you give a tenth of your income to Him, He will give you back more. You may wonder how can I give away money and accumulate. It is because our God is the God of increase. He will take our tenth and multiply it back to us, so you are not losing anything when you give your tithes and offerings, you are gaining.

The book of Hebrews is a letter written to Believers in the new covenant isn't it? As Christians, we are living in this new Blood covenant, but we know that Jesus operated as a prophet under the old covenant when He walked this earth. Through His shed Blood, death and resurrection He not only fulfilled the law but redeemed us from its curse. He ended the old covenant and began the new one. So, when the Bible says "here" mortal men receive tithes, the word "here" is referring to right now or here in the new covenant. Did you hear that? God said He is still receiving tithes from his children in this new covenant. He did not say here mortal men do not receive tithes. He said they receive them. Whom are they receiving tithes for? For God and His work. Some Christians complain about giving their tithes and offerings to a man. I guess they never thought about how they were going to get them to God. Did you think you could give your tithes directly to God? When you give your offerings into different ministries and bring your tithes into your church, you have to put that money into the hands of men. Even in the old covenant they were to put their offering in a basket then hand it to the priest or a mortal man.

"Then the priest shall take the basket out of your hand and set it down before the altar of the Lord your God." (Deuteronomy 26:4)

Again, Hebrews 7:8 says, **"Here mortal men receive tithes, but there he receives them, of whom it is witnessed that he lives."**

It would be nice if Jesus appeared in the flesh so we could hand him our offerings but that is not going to happen. God designed for men and women, who represent Him to receive our tithes and offerings, but even though we give them to men, it is just as real as if God appeared to us and we handed Him our gifts. When the Bible says it is witnessed that He lives, I believe that is talking about Jesus. He is the one who died and arose from the dead and is alive right now. I know Melchizedek is alive in Heaven also, but he is not our high priest. So know this, every time you give your tithes and offerings into the hands of God's ministers, it's Jesus (in Heaven) who is receiving them from you at the very same instant.

That verse said mortal men receive our tithes, it did not say perfect men receive our tithes. If you are waiting for God's ministers to become perfect and to never make any more mistakes, then you will never give again. I know we are perfect in Christ, but we are not experiencing the full manifestation of that perfection yet. The Bible says God demonstrates the excellence of His power through earthen or imperfect vessels. That is all He has to work with. Some Christians are bothered about giving their money to a man, but that is the only way you will be able to get it to God. They will say things like, "I don't know what that preacher is doing with my money." First of all, that is none of your business.

Once your seed leaves your hands it has been sown. Of course, we should not sow our seed just anywhere, but if you believe the Holy Spirit is leading you in your giving then trust Him with your seed and your harvest. When you plant a seed doesn't it have to die to produce a harvest? If you keep wondering what the minister is doing with your tithes, then you are not trusting God as your provider and you are not letting your seed die. You have not fully released your faith in your seed and what it can do. You are still holding onto your seed and therefore hindering the manifestation of your harvest. Also, once you sow your money, it is not "your" money anymore. Quit saying what are they doing with "my money"? It is not your money anymore, so just let it go so it can grow.

I want us to look now at a very big difference in tithing under the law and tithing under grace. Hebrews 7:5 says:

"And indeed those who are of the sons of Levi, who receive the priesthood, have <u>a commandment to receive tithes</u> from the people according to the law, that is, from their brethren, though they have come from the loins of Abraham."

Under the law in the old covenant tithing was a commandment, which is why they <u>paid</u> tithes instead of giving tithes. Abraham <u>gave</u> tithes to Melchizedek, but Levi <u>paid</u> tithes through Abraham. Levi represented the law. That is why they <u>paid</u> tithes, they owed it to God. Even Jesus said it that way to the scribes and Pharisees while He was here operating under the old covenant. The priesthood had not been changed yet and the people were still under the law. Look what the Lord said in Matthew 23:23.

"Woe to you, scribes and Pharisees, hypocrites! For you <u>pay</u> tithe of mint and anise and cumin, and have neglected the weightier

matters of the law: justice and mercy and faith. These you ought to have done, without leaving the others undone."

Jesus was telling them they needed to <u>pay</u> their tithes, but do not forget about justice, mercy and faith. Because they were under the law they still <u>owed</u> God their tithes and Jesus acknowledged that. In Malachi 3:8, 9 God said:

"Will a man rob God? Yet you have robbed Me! But you say, 'In what way have we robbed You?' In tithes and offerings.
You are cursed with a curse, for you have robbed Me, even this whole nation."

Many pastors (and other ministers) will read these verses when it comes time to receive the offering. They will then make this comment, "It is time to <u>pay</u> our tithes. Remember, your tithe belongs to God therefore it is a <u>debt you owe</u>, not a seed you sow. If you don't <u>pay</u> your tithes then you are robbing God and a curse will come on you." If you really think about it, that can inspire more fear than it does faith. We have to operate in faith to receive the harvest from our seed. If we are giving out of fear (fear that a curse may come on us) then we should not be surprised for the lack of harvests we have seen in our finances. That may be a major reason why many of us have not seen more harvests from the seed we have sown. We must give in faith, not in fear!

We know from Hebrews 8:6 that we are in a better covenant which is established on better promises than was the old covenant. Every blessing in the old covenant and much, much more is in the new covenant, but there were instructions about tithing that God gave Israel under the law which do not apply to us today. I know we want to take what God said about tithing under the law and just bring them right over into the new covenant under grace, but if we do that, then grace will not be grace anymore, it will be works. If it becomes works, then we will not have a right to enjoy all that Jesus did for us at Calvary because those blessings are experienced only by faith and freely from God's grace.

In rightly dividing God's Word we need to remember that there are things the Lord spoke to Israel under the law that are still true and important today, and there are some things that do not apply to us today in the new covenant. The law stated that you should not steal and commit adultery, and that is just as true today under grace as it was when God's people were under the law. Under the law they were commanded to give <u>tithes and offerings</u> (not just tithes). If they did not bring those to God, then they were robbing Him. He said they were stealing from Him, which is why it was a debt they owed. The Lord also said that a penalty would accompany stealing from Him. A curse would come on them, so it would be wise to bring their tithes and offerings to Him. Remember, in the old covenant they could not confess that Jesus had redeemed them from the curse. Yes, God would greatly bless them when they obeyed Him, but their tithes and offerings were still debts they owed.

I have heard ministers say today that the tithe (of course in Malachi it said <u>tithes and offerings</u>) is a debt you owe (talking to Believers under grace and not under the law) so until you give God a tenth of your income you are not even sowing any seed. That makes you feel like your tithe is kind of worthless and it will cost you ten percent of your income just to get to where you can sow some "real" seed. Also, I have heard ministers say if you do not bring your tithe into church you are robbing God, but then they will say that anything above the tithe is yours to give as you please. In other words, you are to purpose in your heart when you give an offering because you do not owe that to God, but you cannot purpose in your heart to give your tithe because that is a debt you owe. They are teaching that anything over the tithe is not a debt that you owe. They tell you they are quoting Malachi 3:8, but they are still misquoting it. God told Israel (under the law) they were robbing Him in <u>tithes and offerings</u>, not just tithes. Just because He said to bring the tithes into the storehouse in Malachi 3:10, does not change the fact that He still said (in verse 8) they were robbing Him in <u>tithes and offerings</u>.

Since they were robbing Him in tithes and offerings, then their tithes were not the only debt they owed, their offerings were a debt also. Again, in Malachi 3:8, God said they were robbing Him of tithes <u>and offerings</u>; which would strongly imply that both tithes and offerings belonged to Him wouldn't you agree? If the offerings did not belong to the Lord then He would not have said they robbed Him of tithes <u>and offerings</u>. I think when we read Malachi 3:10 we only zero in on the tithes and kind of forget about what God said concerning the offerings in verse 8.

Of course in this new covenant everything we have and every breath we breathe is from our Heavenly Father, not just our tithes and offerings. After Calvary, our tithes are just as important as they were before Calvary, but under grace we are not commanded to tithe or give. We are told if we sow bountifully we will reap bountifully, and we are also told that we are to purpose in <u>our</u> hearts when we give and to do it cheerfully. The four Gospels are very important books but they are not letters written specifically to the Church. It's true that God's men wrote them after Calvary, but they wrote about what Jesus said while operating in the old covenant. Still Hebrews 7:8 says that the Lord receives our tithes today, so God has not done away with tithing.

Please realize that the way it was under the law and the priesthood of Aaron have changed since Calvary. God changed them in Christ. Hebrews 7:11, 12, 18, 19 says:

"Therefore, if perfection were through the Levitical priesthood (for under it the people received the law), what further need was there that another priest should rise according to the order of Melchizedek, and not be called according to the order of Aaron?

For the priesthood being changed, of necessity there is also a change of the law."

For on the one hand there is an annulling of the former commandment because of its weakness and unprofitableness,

For the law made nothing perfect; on the other hand, there is the bringing in of a better hope, through which we draw near to God."

Because the priesthood has been changed, the law has also been changed. We are under grace in this new covenant, but what does that mean? That means that God finished everything for us in Christ at Calvary. The Lord Jesus obtained eternal redemption for us and paid not only our sin debt, but all of our debts, which would include the tithe and offering debt. Don't tell me that Jesus' precious Blood was powerful enough to pay all sin debt for the entire human race, but could not pay our ten percent tithe debt or any financial debt! I want you to know that Jesus paid off every debt of every kind for you and me! After He arose from the dead, He did not leave us owing anything! We are saved, healed, debt free and eternally redeemed!

Even though we are under grace now, the purpose for our tithes and offerings has not changed. I want to show you several verses.

"And all the tithe of the land, whether of the seed of the land or of the fruit of the tree, is the Lord's. It is holy to the Lord." (Leviticus 27:30)

"Behold, <u>I have given the children of Levi all the tithes</u> in Israel as an inheritance in return for the work which they perform, the work of the tabernacle of meeting." (Numbers 18:21)

"At the end of every third year you shall bring out <u>the tithe</u> of your produce of that year and store it up within your gates.
And the <u>Levite</u>, because he has no portion nor inheritance with you, and the <u>stranger</u> and the <u>fatherless</u> and the <u>widow</u> who are within your gates, may come and eat and be satisfied, that the Lord

your God may bless you in all the work of your hand which you do." (Deuteronomy 14:28, 29)

"And he had prepared for him a large room, where previously they had stored the grain offerings, the frankincense, the articles, <u>the</u> <u>tithes</u> of grain, the new wine and oil, which were commanded to be <u>given to the Levites and singers and gatekeepers</u>, and <u>the offerings for the priests</u>." (Nehemiah 13:5)

The tithe and offerings were to pay and support the Levites or those in the ministry. They were also to be used to bless and help the stranger, fatherless, widows, singers, gatekeepers and the priests. In other words, they were to be used to support the work of the ministry. In Malachi 3:10 God told us where to bring our tithes, and it was into the storehouse. He said that the storehouse was a place where there would be food to feed His people. He was talking about natural food then and that is still true today. Feeding the poor did not cease with the old covenant. But the main food God's ministers are to feed His people is spiritual food (the Word of God). The number one place where God's people are fed is in the local church. I believe it is very important that we bring our tithes into our local church for that very reason. God has not done away with the ministry or the feeding of His sheep, therefore, our tithes and offerings are very vital and important.

The tithe is not a debt we owe, but the purpose for the tithe is just as important now, if not more important than it was in the old covenant. A major purpose for our tithes and offerings is to financially enable God's ministers to preach the Gospel throughout the earth and win the lost to Jesus. Therefore, bringing our tithes and offerings to the Lord is how we honor God and His work (Proverbs 3:9)!

Let me tell you another reason why it is important to give our tithes and offerings. Obviously, God does not need any money, He is doing fine, but here is how we can rob God in the New Covenant. If we decide not to sow our financial seed, then we are robbing God of a great blessing. I know you are probably wondering, "How can we rob God of a blessing?" Our Heavenly Father is a real Father, and He wants to bless us. He wants to experience the joy and pleasure of seeing His children enjoying His goodness, just like any parent would. According to the law of sowing and reaping, we must sow our seed or our Father cannot give us a harvest of blessings to enjoy; therefore, we have robbed Him of the joy and delight in blessing His children. If you had plenty of money and your children would not allow you to give them anything, that would rob you of great joy and pleasure wouldn't it? So, let's quit robbing God! Let's please our Father God by expecting to sow more seed and reap bigger harvests!

Jesus also redeemed (freed) us from the curse of the law (Galatians 3:13, 14)! There is not any curse that will come on us if we do not tithe! Now listen! Yes, we are redeemed from the curse of the law, but we are not redeemed from the curse of disobedience. The Lord said if you sow to the flesh you will reap corruption and if you sow to the Spirit you will of the Spirit reap life everlasting (Galatians 6:7-9). God's Kingdom operates according to the law of seedtime and harvest. If you want to actually experience and enjoy what Jesus has already done for you, obedience to God's spiritual laws of seedtime and harvest, His law of faith, law of the Spirit of Life in Christ Jesus and law of love are still necessary, but we are to operate in these supernatural laws of God's Kingdom because we purpose in our hearts to, not because of a command from the law.

As we operate in faith, we do it from a place of knowing that God has already done everything for us in Christ. So, when we give, we are not doing it to get God to give us something, but we are giving as a way to release our faith to receive or experience what God has already given us in Christ. Even though we are not under the law, seedtime and harvest have never changed. If you want a financial harvest you still must sow financial seed, and even though (while under grace) you are not commanded to give, it would still be a very wise decision. If you choose not to be a cheerful giver into the work of the Lord that is your choice, but you may end up living your life as though you were not redeemed from the curse of the law.

The blessings of Heaven do not automatically materialize in our lives just because we are Christians. Faith must be released, which is sowing seed. Tithes and offerings must be sown, which is sowing seed. Time invested in praying, reading and studying God's Word must be sown, which is also sowing seed. You can't get away from the seed, so learn how to become proficient in sowing them; that is how the Kingdom operates. If you were a farmer, you do not <u>have to</u> sow any tomato seeds, but if you want a tomato harvest you had better get to planting. You may not have to sow corn seed, but you will not get a corn harvest if you don't! Just because you do not have to tithe (since you are under grace) does not change the fact that if you want to prosper financially you must sow financial seed. Seedtime and harvest did not quit working when we got saved and came under God's grace. The Lord said while the earth remains seedtime and harvest shall not cease (Genesis 8:22)! God said that before the law was ever given.

So the question in tithing and giving is not do I have to, but do I love God and trust Him as my provider. Do I want to honor God, do I want to be a financial channel for the Gospel, and do I want to experience God's blessings for me and my family? Now, do you see how we have been asking the wrong question? Tithing and giving under grace means that we never have to give out of fear or obligation, but always out of love and joy. Therefore, when we go to church we can look forward to offering time.

I want to bring up one more thing for you to think about before we move on to the next chapter, but you will need a good understanding about the authority of the Believer to see this. Malachi 3:10, 11 says:

"Bring all the tithes into the storehouse, that there may be food in My house, and try Me now in this, says the Lord of hosts, If I will not open for you the windows of heaven and pour out for you such blessing that there will not be room enough to receive it.

And I will rebuke the devourer for your sakes, so that he will not destroy the fruit of your ground, nor shall the vine fail to bear fruit for you in the field, says the Lord of Hosts."

The Bible tells <u>me</u> to resist the devil doesn't it? So let me ask you a question? Why would I need to do that if God does it for me? Have you ever thought about that? One minister said he was rebuking the devil one day when the Lord spoke to him. He said that the Lord ask him what he was doing, and he told Him he was rebuking the devil. According to this minister, he said the Lord told him that he did not need to rebuke the devil because he was a tither. I believe God can speak to us and we should expect to hear His voice, but just because this minister said he heard from the Lord does not mean he did. Did you know you can think you are hearing from God when you are actually hearing from your own spirit? You may not have thought about this, but sometimes what comes up within us is not God speaking but its things we have been taught. We are actually hearing them over again in our hearts and minds. We think we are hearing from God and we are simply hearing messages coming up out of our spirit that others have taught us; that is why we need to examine by God's Word what we read and hear.

I know it sounds good to believe that God is rebuking the devil for us, and I am not about to say He can't do that. I gladly welcome Him to do that if He wants to, but that is not what God teaches us in the new covenant. God can do anything He wants to, but He will never do anything contrary to His Word. He and His Word are one. Let me tell you what His Word says in the new covenant.

"<u>Nor give place</u> to the devil.</u>" (Ephesians 4:27) It is up to you and me not to give the devil any place; God will not do it for us. The Amplified Bible says:

"Leave no [such] room or foothold for the devil [give no opportunity to him]."

"Therefore submit to God. <u>Resist the devil and he will flee from you.</u>" (James 4:7)

We are the ones who have to resist the devil; God will not do it for us.

"Be sober, be vigilant; because your adversary the devil walks about like a roaring lion, seeking whom he may devour.
<u>Resist him</u>, steadfast in the faith, knowing that the same sufferings are experienced by your brotherhood in the world." (I Peter 5:8, 9)

Once again, we have to resist the devil; God will not do it for us. If it was up to Him, he would not have told us to do it.

"We know that whoever is born of God does not sin; but he who has been born of God <u>keeps himself</u>, and the wicked one does not touch him." (I John 5:18)

And again, we have to keep or guard ourselves and the wicked one will not touch us. We cannot live and act any way we want to and think that God will keep the devil off our backs! I know that God is also our protector but we also have a responsibility. There is not any Scripture in the letters to the Church which says God will resist and rebuke the devil for us, why? Why is it different now than it was in the old covenant? In the old covenant they could not be born again, Jesus had not yet defeated the devil and they did not have the kind of authority and power we have in Christ as the redeemed. They could not say to the devil, "I am God's righteousness in Christ and you have no place in me! I conquered you through Jesus' death and resurrection, so get out of my life!" They needed God to rebuke the devil for them. They did not have the kind of redemption rights and privileges we have now; that is why this is a better covenant with better promises.

If you think about it, even the angels do not have the same authority and power we have in Christ. When Michael the archangel (Jude 9) was contending with the devil he said the Lord rebuke you. Our Heavenly Father (because we are sons, and angels are not sons of God) never told us to say the Lord rebuke you. As you can see from the Word, He told **us** out right to resist the devil. Jesus told all Believers, in Mark 16:17, to cast out demons! He did not say when you come upon the devil you need to say the Lord rebuke you. Yes, it is in His authority that we cast out demons and rebuke the devil, but we are to speak to the devil in Jesus' Name and command him to leave! We are to resist him and he has to obey us in the Name of the Lord!

I don't like it when I am trying to stand by faith on a certain Scripture but I feel like something is not quite right or something is missing in my understanding, and this is where I have done that for years, believing that God is rebuking the devourer or the devil for me because I am a tither, while at the same time thinking, "Then why do I need to resist the devil?" Why would God need my help if being a tither would take care of it? It doesn't make sense if God only rebukes the devil when I tithe then all the rest of the time I must rebuke him. Does the rebuke of Almighty God run out of power at some point so it is up to me to take up the slack? Is there some kind of time limit on how long God's rebuke will last? Can we say that God's rebuke will last for six days after you tithe, and then you have to begin rebuking the devil yourself? That sounds silly doesn't it? Can you see how hard it is reconciling God rebuking the devil for me with what He clearly instructed me to do in this new covenant. I could not fit the two together; that's because they do not go together. One applies to the old covenant under the law and the other one applies to the new covenant under grace. God's Word cannot contradict itself.

I want to remind you about the vision Kenneth Hagin Sr. had many years ago. The Lord was teaching him about the authority of the Believer. In this vision Jesus appeared to brother Hagin and started talking to him, but while He was talking a little demon spirit came between them and started jumping up and down, making a lot of noise. Brother Hagin said it was irritating because he could not hear what the Lord was saying. He was also wondering why the Lord did not make the demon leave. Finally, in a strong voice, Kenneth Hagin commanded the demon to leave in Jesus' Name and he left! Now here is where we got some great revelation on the authority of the Believer.

Kenneth Hagin asked the Lord, why He did not make the demon leave. To his amazement, Jesus said He <u>could not</u> make him leave. Brother Hagin said, "Didn't you mean that you <u>would not</u> make him leave?" The Lord said no I did not say I would not, I said that I could not. Even though the Lord told him three times that He could not make the demon leave, brother Hagin still did not understand why. He said that what the Lord told him greatly messed up his theology because he had never heard that before. He also told Jesus, even though I am looking at you right now, I still cannot use this experience as my final authority. Your Word is my final authority, so I will need you to give me at least 3 witnesses (Scriptures) out of the New Testament to prove that. Jesus ended up giving him 4 different witnesses. The Lord taught him and us as well, that if we do not like what the devil is doing then we have to rebuke him in Jesus' Name! When I was thinking about this story, this question came to mind, "Why didn't Jesus tell brother Hagin that He (God) would rebuke the devil for him, since he was a tither?" Well, we should know the answer to that question by now.

You never ignore Scriptures in the new covenant to obey Scriptures in the old one. If something does not seem like it fits correctly between the old and new testaments, then we are experiencing an attack of ignorance on our behalf. We need to recognize that we are missing some truth here that we do not see and we need to ask the Lord to open up our spiritual eyes so we can see. I would be very glad for God to rebuke the devil for me when I tithe, I would not reject that at all, but that still does not exempt you and me from resisting the devil and casting him out in Jesus' Name. We know from the New Testament Scriptures that resisting and rebuking the devil and his demons is something the Lord told us to do. Let me remind you of what God said to the Apostle Paul in II Corinthians 12:7-9.

"And lest I should be exalted above measure by the abundance of the revelations, a thorn in the flesh was given to me, a messenger of Satan to buffet me, lest I be exalted above measure.

Concerning this thing I pleaded with the Lord three times that it might depart from me.

And He said to me, 'My grace is sufficient for you, for My strength is made perfect in weakness.' Therefore, most gladly I will rather boast in my

infirmities, that the power of Christ may rest upon me."

The Bible says that Paul pleaded with the Lord three times to get rid of the demon spirit harassing him. The thorn was not some disease, it was a messenger of Satan sent (not by God) to buffet Paul. God gave Paul a lot of revelation about Jesus and what He finished for us at Calvary. Jesus said in Mark, chapter four, when talking about the parable of the sower, that when people hear the Word (revelation) then the devil comes immediately to steal it. The devil tried his hardest to stop Paul from acting on the Word he received, and he also tried his best to stop Paul from teaching that Word to the Church. If you noticed in those verses, Paul did not say, "Lord you know I am a tither, so why haven't you rebuked the devil for me?" The Lord told him that His grace was more than enough. That was another way of saying that <u>you</u> need to do something about the devil.

Well what is God's grace? We all know it is His favor, but it is also the operation of His power in our lives. In essence, God told Paul that he had to resist the devil. He had given Paul all of the grace he needed to rebuke the devil in Jesus' Name! If you read the last two verses (especially the last four words) at the end of the book of Acts, you will see that the messenger of Satan was gone. I believe what we have talked about is very important because many Christians may start believing they don't need to resist the devil anymore because they are tithers. Once again, being a tither does not exempt you from obeying the New Testament Scriptures and resisting and rebuking the devil in Jesus' Name.

I pray that you will receive the Word of God you have read in this chapter about tithing and that you will take time to meditate and study all of these Scriptures. We all need to stay open to what the Holy Spirit wants to teach us no matter what we think we already know. When the Lord began to open up my eyes to some things I had not seen about tithing, I almost rejected it because it did not agree with what I had been taught for the last 40 years. It is good to be quick to defend the Word of God you believe, but be honest enough to examine what you believe with the Scriptures to make sure you believe correctly.

It is not good enough to say that you believe a certain way because that was the way you were taught, or because your denomination teaches it that way, or because most preachers teach it that way, or because that is the way I have always taught it. The question you should continually ask is, what does the Word of God say about what I believe? Let's not allow pride to hinder us from being pruned to produce more fruit (John 15:1, 2). You can see why I was quick not to accept what I heard, but I decided to listen anyway. I began meditating on these Scriptures in a new light than I had previously experienced. I began to study and check them out with other verses in the Bible. Now, I am not quick to jump on the band wagon when I hear something "new". Many times what is "new" is not new at all, it just seems new to me or to you. I always examine everything I read and hear with the Word of God. I am not looking for some "new revelation" that no one has ever heard before, but at the same time if I need to be corrected in my theology then I should be open and willing to receive whatever changes the Spirit of God wants to make in my life, how about you?

I am so glad that in this wonderful new Blood covenant we can tithe and give cheerfully as we purpose in our hearts. We are not giving out of fear that a curse will come on us and we are not giving because it is a continual debt we owe to God. We have the freedom under grace not to give, so now, we can look forward to giving and we can hardly wait to give again. We are not trying anymore to get our tithes "paid". I believe that when you get a hold of what we have studied in this chapter, tithing will never be a difficulty again. You will never think of giving less than ten percent. You will not be secretly hoping you could give less, but your desire will be just the opposite. You will joyfully and always want to give much more than the tithe, so let's have fun sowing and reaping! I look forward to giving my tithes and offerings at church and to becoming new financial partners with other ministries!

CHAPTER
7

ARE YOU WILLING TO PROSPER?

Are you really sure you are <u>willing</u> to prosper? I don't just mean are you sure you would like a new car or are you sure you would like all your bills paid. Look with me at Isaiah 1:19, 20.

"If you are <u>willing</u> and <u>obedient</u>, you shall eat the good of the land;
But if you refuse and rebel, you shall be devoured by the sword."

If you noticed in this verse, the prophet used the words <u>willing</u> and <u>obedient</u>. One translation says if you will willingly obey. I believe that takes away from what the Lord wants us to see here about these two words. I believe it's more than asking will you "willingly obey". That still sounds like the writer is emphasizing only being obedient. Also God's prophet did not ask if you would be willing <u>or</u> obedient. He said we must be willing <u>and</u> obedient. The Lord brought my attention to this almost 40 years ago while listening to a cassette tape by Kenneth Hagin Senior. He was talking about the early days of his ministry and how they were struggling financially. He was obeying God and travelling everywhere the Lord wanted him to go minister. One day he began to talk to the Lord about Isaiah 1:19, and why he and his family were suffering financially.

He said that he pleaded his case with the Lord and told Him that he was obeying and doing all that He called him to do, but he still was not eating the good of the land. He said his kids were not adequately dressed, the tires on his old car were bald and he really was not prospering like he should be. He said the Lord spoke to him and said your problem is you have not been practicing what you preach. Brother Hagin said, "Lord you hit me a low blow. I have been practicing what I preach. I have been doing everything you told me to do." He said the Lord agreed with him that he had been very obedient, but told him he hadn't been much <u>willing</u>. When I heard that I realized there is a difference between the words willing and obedient. Did you know you can be willing and not obedient, and you can be obedient and not willing? You can tell your child to clean his room and he may say I will, but then not do it. He is willing but not obedient, or your child may say I will not clean my room, but in a few minutes he cleans it. This time he was obedient but not willing.

Kenneth Hagin said the Lord told him he was obedient, and he was doing everything he was called to do, but he wasn't much willing. When I heard about what the Lord told brother Hagin it really got my attention. I have some understanding of how greatly God used brother Hagin (from his writings and teachings) and if he missed it back then and wasn't willing, it occurred to me that I might need to examine my life to see if I am genuinely willing and obedient. Brother Hagin said he made an adjustment in his spirit and told the Lord that he was now willing. God began to teach him about financial prosperity and he started eating the good of the land.

Now let me say this about works. I know that good works are very important and they should be the outcome of faith in our hearts. Of course I am talking about works of faith here, not works of the law; but also don't forget that God looks on the heart of man doesn't He? Being obedient is expressed in our works, but being willing reveals the motives and attitudes of the heart. It means we are willing to obey God and do His will. I want to look at III John 2 again and touch on a few more things we discussed in chapter one because these two chapters really complement each other.

"Beloved, I pray that you may prosper in all things and be in health, just as your soul prospers."

Always remember that God's will is His Word and His Word is His will. God and His Word are one (John 1:1). If you want to know what God's will is for your life, read His Word. If you want to know what God's will is concerning your health, read His Word. If you want to know what His will is concerning your prosperity, read His Word. The Lord made it very clear in His Word that His will for us is to prosper in all (which includes financial and material prosperity) things, walk in perfect health even as we prosper spiritually. Since that is God's will for our total being, then we should be willing to do that. God's will is for all His children to prosper financially. Are you willing to do that? I ask that question because there are ministers who have vowed a vow of poverty. Now, does that sound like they are willing to prosper? No, it doesn't. Many of these ministers think they are being spiritual and humble, but they are not. Being broke is not a sign of spirituality or humility. It is a sign of ignorance to God's will for their lives. They are actually not submitting to the will of God for their finances, and they are not being willing and obedient.

Let me share with you the Hebrew definition of the word willing. **It means to rest content and to be acquiescent.** Please don't let the word acquiescent bother you because it is a good word. **It means to be ready to accept something without protest, or to do what someone else wants.** By vowing a vow of poverty, they are protesting God's will for their finances. They are not willing to do what God wants. They are not willing to prosper and they are actually hiding their unwillingness in the guise of humility. Or you could say it this way; they are not willing to acquiesce to III John 2.

As Christians, we are taught to submit our wills to God's will, and to always declare, "not our will but His will be done." You may want to drive a bicycle everywhere you go, but what if God wills for you to drive a nice car, are you going to acquiesce to His will? Are you going to submit to His will? Are you willing to accept more prosperity, even though you really did not want it? Why would your Heavenly Father want you to drive a nice car? Of course it gives Him great pleasure to see you blessed, but it's also a great testimony to the world that you serve the Most High God and He loves and provides for you. Even if you do not want much for yourself, be willing to prosper any way to give God pleasure, and to be a more convincing testimony to the world of His goodness (Psalm 35:27).

A pastor was telling me the story of a great man of God that lived a long time ago. This man used his faith over the years to feed probably thousands of orphans. He believed God for thousands of dollars a month to do that. According to this pastor, this man of God always had just enough to feed and clothe the children, but never any left over for himself. This pastor acted thrilled and amazed at how God was able to fully supply everything needed for the ministry while seemingly keeping this man broke at the same time. Twice the pastor reiterated how God gave that minister plenty of money to feed the poor, but personally speaking he did not have much for himself. I was amazed at how this pastor seemed to think that it was a wonderful miracle for this minister to have plenty of money for the ministry but none to speak of for his family.

Please hear me now! God is not opposed to His children being rich (I Timothy 6:17!), He is opposed to His children being covetous. As I mentioned before, you can be covetous as a millionaire and you can be covetous while flat broke. Let me say this also, unselfishness is not measured by how little or much money and things you have. We are talking about attitudes of the heart. That is why Jesus told us to seek His Kingdom and righteousness <u>first</u>, then all these other things (especially financial and material blessings) would be added (not subtracted) unto us (Matthew 6:33).

Again, the response from the pastor telling me the story about feeding the orphans further demonstrates how many ministers do not understand what it means to be willing and obedient. As a minister, it is not

God's will that you have just enough money to pay all of the ministry bills, but not enough to pay your personal bills. The testimony about feeding the orphans is great, but not as great as it could be. I do praise God that this minister had plenty of money for the children, but it would have been a greater testimony if the world of unbelievers saw him enjoying all of God's blessings as well! God can do both! Do not settle for one or the other! The testimony that causes the world to see how much God loves us and that we are the blessed of the Lord is His overflowing goodness in our personal lives.

One of God's Names is El Shaddai, and it means God almighty, the God who is more than enough. God does not want you and me to not have enough. He does not want us to have just enough. He wants and expects us to have <u>more than enough</u>! Remember what El Shaddai told Abraham in Genesis 12:2, 3?

"I will make you a great nation; <u>I will bless you</u> and make your name great; and <u>you shall be a blessing</u>.
I will bless those who bless you, and I will curse him who curses you; and in you all the families of the earth shall be blessed."

God did not tell Abraham, "I want you personally to vow a vow of poverty because I do not want you to have anything, and even though you will not enjoy my blessings, I will still give you plenty to bless others with." God let Abraham know that He was El Shaddai and He had plenty to bless Abraham and his family with more than enough, and plenty over and above that so Abraham could generously bless others! Let me show you the results of the blessing of the Lord on Abraham's personal life. Genesis 13:2 says: **"Abram was <u>very rich</u> in livestock, in silver, and in gold."** He wasn't just rich spiritually and physically, but also financially and materially. I believe that God wanted this minister we were talking about (who fed the orphans) to not only use his faith so the orphans would have plenty but also for him and his family to have plenty. I believe that God wants you and me to believe Him for plenty for our families and for His Kingdom work. That is simple for our God to do isn't it? I think you would be blessed even more if you would go back and read the first chapter of this book a few more times. Quit thinking that you have to do without so there will be enough for the Kingdom! El Shaddai is a lot bigger than that! God wants you living in abundant prosperity, yes abundant life (John 10:10), and having plenty to support the proclamation of the Gospel!

To be willing is to see <u>you</u> prosperous. When you are truly willing, then you will see yourself prosperous before your bills are paid off. Just like healing, if you are convinced that healing is God's will for you, then you will see it done (in your spirit) before you feel it done in your body. That's what faith is. You see it done, before it is done in the natural realm. Farmers have been doing this for a long time. They would take you out to their field and show you where their green beans are, where their tomatoes are, where their cucumbers are, where their corn is, as well as everything else they planted. They would point to the dirt and show you where all of their different vegetables are, before anything has come forth. All you see out there is dirt, but they don't, they see all those different vegetables.

In other words, all you would see is dirt, but yet they see vegetables. Why do they see green beans, corn, etc.? I know with their natural eyes they don't see these vegetables already sprouting, but you could say that they already envision their harvests because of the seed they have sown. Since you have not sown any seed there, you don't see or expect a harvest, but they do. When you have really sown your faith as a seed for your healing, then you will see (through your eyes of faith) yourself healed, even though you do not feel it yet. When you get the revelation (which is being willing) that you are already financially rich in Christ (II Corinthians 8:9) and you have given your tithes and offerings, then you will not be stressed, afraid or troubled anymore about finances. You will see all your bills paid and plenty of money in the bank before you see it in the natural realm. You will not struggle anymore because you know that God is your source and you trust Him to bring your harvests to pass. Remember, you are not giving your tithes and offerings to get God to bless you, because He has already done that by His grace in Christ. You are giving your tithes and offerings simply to receive into the natural realm what He has already blessed you with. You could say that is how you make withdrawals out of the finished work of Christ. Let me remind you of a great faith building story about Caleb and Joshua in Numbers 13.

"And the Lord spoke to Moses, saying, 'Send men to spy out the land of Canaan, which I am giving to the children of Israel; from each tribe of their fathers you shall send a man, everyone a leader among them.'

And they returned from spying out the land after forty days.

Then they told him, and said: 'We went to the land where you sent us. It truly flows with milk and honey, and this is its fruit.

Nevertheless, the people who dwell in the land are strong; the cities are fortified and very large; moreover, we saw the descendants of Anak there. (Numbers 13:1, 2, 27, 28, 30, 31)

Then Caleb quieted the people before Moses, and said, 'Let us go up at once and take possession, for we are well able to overcome it.

But the men who had gone up with him said, 'We are not able to go up against the people, for they are stronger than we.'" (Numbers 13:1, 2, 27-28, 30-31)

God told them He was giving them the land, a land of abundant prosperity, but ten of the twelve spies were not willing and obedient. They were not willing to eat the good of the land. Can you see how they were not willing to prosper? In this case, because they were not willing to prosper and because they could not see themselves living in the land of plenty, they chose not to obey God; therefore, they did not eat the good of the land. So, I want to ask you again, are you sure you are willing and obedient? It takes faith to eat the good of the land! It takes faith to possess your possessions (Obadiah 17)!

The devil absolutely hates it when you have plenty of money! He does not want you to be healthy because then you can go and preach the Gospel, but when you have plenty of money, you can not only go preach, but now you can pay for many others to go and preach the Gospel around the world! That is why the devil loves to hear Christians say, "I don't need much money. I am satisfied with what I have. What in the world would I do with thousands of dollars coming into me every month?" Those Christians need to get God's vision! They don't see the world like God does! They really don't understand that God's Kingdom is much bigger than their little local church! It is more than just believing God to have enough money for gas to go to church on Sunday and come home!

I praise God for those who attend your local church, but there are millions, if not billions of more people that need to hear the Gospel! It will take a lot of money to preach the Word to all of these people. God wants to use you and me in doing that. Let's start developing and stretching our faith to believe in thousands of dollars to finance ministries which are taking the Gospel into all the world! We are God's mouth pieces and His hands extended! The truth is, these small vision minded Christians can't see past themselves, and they are usually the ones complaining about why there are so many ministers preaching on prosperity! They need to repent, submit and acquiesce to God's will for their lives!! The Lord wants every Believer to be a great financial channel for His Kingdom! Now look with me at a few more verses in the book of Numbers.

"But Joshua the son of Nun and Caleb the son of Jephunneth, who were among those who had spied out the land, tore their clothes;

And they spoke to all the congregation of the children of Israel, saying: 'The land we passed through to spy out is an exceedingly good land.

If the Lord delights in us, then He will bring us into this land and give it to us, a land which flows with milk and honey.

Only do not rebel against the Lord, nor fear the people of the land, for they are our bread; their protection has departed from them, and the Lord is with us. Do not fear them.'

And all the congregation said to stone them with stones. Now the glory of the Lord appeared in the tabernacle of meeting before all the children of Israel." (Numbers 14: 6-10)

Verse 9 said they (10 of the spies) feared the people of the land. Let me say it in a little different way. They were afraid to prosper. I know there are many people who are afraid of losing their money, they are afraid of losing their job and they are afraid of not having enough, but there are also those who are actually afraid to prosper. They don't know how to handle it, they don't want the responsibility that comes with increase and they don't want to deal with what others (especially family members) may say. But I praise the Lord for the faith of Joshua and Caleb! They were willing and obedient weren't they? They were not afraid to succeed and experience everything God promised them. When you are truly willing and obedient you will see through eyes of faith. You will see what God sees and you will know what God wants you to know about the situation. It does not matter what giants are in your land! It does not matter how the economy is! It does not matter what demons of fear, doubt, sickness or poverty are in your land! God has given the land to you, so you can run all of your enemies out of it in Jesus' Name!! But you have to be willing to do that! You have to be willing to prosper, willing to succeed in all that God has called you to do! You have to be willing to possess and occupy (for the Kingdom of God) all the land the Lord has promised you.

I recently heard a minister say, "I don't pay for anything, but I believe God for everything." The point being, it is not about how much money I have in the bank, but how much does God have. Yes, God pays for things through me, but it all comes from Him. In other words, it doesn't matter what it cost because God can afford it; therefore, I can afford it in Christ. Since all things are possible to him who believes, then it is not about how much money I have. It is not about how expensive something is. Nothing is too expensive for the Lord, and since we are in Christ, nothing is too expensive for us. So, it's not about what will I have to pay for this. It is about what I can believe God for. We are heirs of God and joint heirs with Jesus! In Christ we are far beyond billionaires! All that I am talking about here has to do with being willing.

If you were a billionaire (in the natural realm) you probably would never think about costs nor would you wonder if you could afford something. Why? Because you see yourself wealthy, and you cannot see yourself any other way. We (the Church) need to see ourselves not only healthy but wealthy, and we need to get up every day expecting to experience more and more of all that God has given us in· Christ! We need it all right now on this earth, so expect it to come to pass in your life! That is being willing and obedient!

Now, I want you to notice something in the last verse we read in Numbers 14:10. The Bible said <u>the entire</u> congregation wanted to stone Joshua and Caleb. Did you know there are people that will not like you prospering; especially when you have more than they do? They will be jealous of course, but remember that Jesus said (in Mark 10:29, 30) with the hundred-fold return would also come persecution. That is another reason why I am asking the question again, "Are you sure you are willing?"

This should not be a difficult question to answer. If your heart is to glorify God above everything else, to fulfill His calling on your life and to experience all that Jesus accomplished for you at Calvary, then this will be a very easy question to answer. Let me give you one more verse that compliments Isaiah 1:19.

"If they obey and serve Him, they shall spend their days in prosperity, and their years in pleasures." (Job 36: 11)

He did not say they will spend their days in lack and their years in sadness. Why? Because that is not God's will for His people! God wants you to eat the good, wear the good, drive the good, live in the good and have plenty of the good to give to others!

CHAPTER
8

IMPARTATION THROUGH PARTNERSHIP

A number of years ago I heard Kenneth Copeland share his testimony of when He and Gloria became financial partners with Oral Roberts. Apparently, Oral Roberts was receiving an offering and giving everyone the opportunity to become financial partners with him for $10.00 a month. Brother Copeland said that someone ended up giving him $10.00 so he could become a partner as well. He said their partnership with Oral Roberts came about many years ago when they were struggling financially and had just begun learning about the things of God. Now here is what got my attention when I heard this story. Brother Copeland said that when he arrived home from the meeting and greeted Gloria, one of the first things he said to her was, "We just got Oral Roberts anointing for $10.00 a month!" Suddenly, when I heard him say that, I saw financial partnership with ministries in a new and greater light! Of course I know you cannot buy God's Anointing for any amount of money, and I know brother Copeland was not talking about buying the

Anointing. He was talking about impartation through partnership. There is so much we can receive by becoming financial partners with men and women of God. Let's start by looking at Philippians 4: 15-20.

15. "Now you Philippians know also that in the beginning of the gospel, when I departed from Macedonia, no church shared with me concerning giving and receiving but you only.

16. For even in Thessalonica you sent aid once and again for my necessities.

17. Not that I seek the gift, but I seek the fruit that abounds to your account.

18. Indeed I have all and abound. I am full, having received from Epaphroditus the things sent from you, a sweet-smelling aroma, an acceptable sacrifice, well pleasing to God.

19. And my God shall supply all your need according to His riches in glory by Christ Jesus.

20. Now to our God and Father be glory forever and ever. Amen.

Philippians 4:19 is probably one of the main Scriptures that most Christians like to confess, but for many it doesn't seem to be working. Now, the Word always works. If it seems to you that it is not working, then don't blame God's Word. It is never the Word's fault! Examine what you are believing and doing to see where you missed it. God will supply all your need, but you need to realize there is a big contingency which accompanies that verse. There is a responsibility which you must fulfill to rightly claim that promise. You have to realize that verse nineteen is connected to other verses in chapter four.

According to verse 15, the Apostle Paul was talking to the Believers in Philippi who were givers into his ministry. You might say they were financial partners with the Apostle Paul. He said they shared with him in giving and receiving once and again. It was to these Believers that Paul said my God will supply all your need. If you are not a tither and giver in God's Kingdom then you don't have a right to expect Philippians 4:19 to work for you. You could say that Philippians 4:19 is the harvest from the seed we sow. Paul knew and understood about sowing and reaping. He knew that God's Kingdom operates according to seedtime and harvest. I believe he was telling his financial partners in Philippi that because they had sown into his ministry, now God will supply everything they need.

Once again, sowing our financial seed is not how we get God to supply our need. We are not trying to get God to do anything for us! He has already done everything for us through Jesus' precious Blood! Sowing our seed is our faith response to what the Lord has already given us so we can now receive or experience it in our lives.

Many Christians are confessing that God will supply all their need, but they have not sown anything. Let's make this real simple. If a farmer confessed every day that God will supply him with a corn harvest, but refuses to sow corn seed, will God still supply his need of a corn harvest? No! Even though he has a good confession and he is standing on Philippians 4:19, he is still not obeying a major Kingdom law called seedtime and harvest. Remember, God said that seedtime and harvest shall not cease as long as the earth remains. If you want a harvest or if you want God to meet your needs, you must sow some seeds. Remember, I am talking about God manifesting for you what is already yours in Christ.

Paul told these Philippians in verse seventeen that he did not seek a gift from them, but he sought fruit that would abound to their account. I like what Pastor Leroy Thompson says, "I did not come to get money from you, I came to get money to you." But the way for God to get money and all kinds of blessings to you, is for you to sow some seed. Listen now to Philippians 4:15-17 out of the Amplified Bible.

"And you Philippians yourselves well know that in the early days of the Gospel ministry, when

I left Macedonia, no church (assembly) entered into partnership with me and opened up [a debit and credit] account in giving and receiving except you only.

For even in Thessalonica you sent [me contributions] for my needs, not only once but a second time.

Not that I seek or am eager for [your] gift, but I do seek and am eager for the fruit which increases to your credit [the harvest of blessing that is accumulating to your account]."

I like the fact that the Amplified Bible referred to the Philippians account as a debit and credit account. The Lord Jesus talked about laying up for ourselves treasures in Heaven, or in our Heavenly account (Matthew 6:19-21). Whenever we give into God's work, we are making deposits into our Heavenly account, and we can also make withdrawals from our Heavenly account while on this earth. The Lord told us a great benefit of having a Heavenly account. He said moth and rust cannot destroy and thieves cannot break in and steal what we have on deposit in our Heavenly account. The economy, stock market and world conditions have no effect on our Heavenly account. If you are a tither and a giver, you never have to worry about your needs being met, and you never have to worry about what the economy is doing! You have an account which is out of this world that you can make withdrawals from while living in this world.

Many times Christians are confessing Psalm 23:1, the Lord is my shepherd and I shall not want or lack, but if they are not sowers then their confession will not have any substance to it. Do you see this? When God sent Elijah to the widow woman in I Kings chapter seventeen, he told her that she needed to sow some seed. He did not tell her that all she needed to do was to keep confessing the Lord is my shepherd and I shall not want. I believe this is one of the areas where we have missed it in the past, and failed to experience great financial prosperity. Especially when it comes to finances, our good confession needs to be accompanied with financial seed. Now let's look at some other things about financial partnership. Philippians 1:7 says:

"Just as it is right for me to think this of you all, because I have you in my heart, inasmuch as both in my chains and in the defense and confirmation of the gospel, <u>you all are partakers with me of grace</u>."

We read in chapter four how there were Christians at Philippi who were financial partners (sowers) in the ministry of the Apostle Paul. It was these Christians that Paul considered partakers with him of grace. I don't believe we have fully tapped into the kind of harvest God desires to give us through partnership with other ministries. Do you remember Elisha getting a double portion of the anointing on Elijah. You could also say he got to partake of a double portion of the grace on Elijah. Theologians tell us that Elisha probably followed Elijah for 15 to 20 years before he received the double portion. Most of us do not have the time to follow anther minister around for 20 years, but one thing we can do that does not require traveling all over the world is to be his or her financial partner.

Sowing money into ministries of God is actually spiritual. I know the money itself is natural, but the giving of it is a spiritual act. You may ask why? Through your financial seed God is connecting you with His grace, gifts and anointing's. Paul said that to his Philippian partners. He said they were partaking with him of grace, or of the same grace he was operating in. I find it very interesting that the Holy Spirit through Paul chose to talk about partaking of grace. Paul knew a lot about grace didn't he? Again, what is grace? It is the operation of God's power. Within God's grace are all the blessings and benefits we have in Christ. Through our financial seed we have the privilege of experiencing the same power, blessings and anointing's that are operating in the lives of the ministers we support. I am not saying if you give to an apostle you will become an apostle, but, we can expect to minister in greater salvation, revelation, healing, miracle and financial anointing's. Let me give you some more Scriptures on this.

"Then He got into one of the boats, which was Simon's, and asked him to put out a little from the land. And He sat down and taught the multitudes from the boat.

When He had stopped speaking, He said to Simon, 'Launch out into the deep and let down your nets for a catch.'

But Simon answered and said to Him, 'Master, we have toiled all night and caught nothing; nevertheless, at Your word I will let down the net.'

And when they had done this, they caught a great number of fish, and their net was breaking.

So they signaled to <u>their partners</u> in the other boat to come and help them. And they came and <u>filled both the boats</u>, so that they began to sink." (Luke 5:3-7)

What a great story and what a great miracle! Here is what especially got my attention. Peter's <u>partners</u> experienced the same financial blessing, or the same grace that Peter experienced. By allowing the Lord to use his boat, he was sowing it as a seed into Jesus' ministry, and then the Lord told him how to reap a harvest from it.

Peter's partners did not sow the same seed he sowed, but they got to reap the same harvest! Praise God for partnership! Peter's boat was full of fish and his partner's boat was full of fish. That sounds like what the Apostle Paul said about partaking with him of grace doesn't it? Now you know what Kenneth Copeland meant when he said, "We just got Oral Roberts anointing for $10.00 a month!" He got a revelation of partnership didn't he? Do you have a revelation of partnership? I hope you do. Leia and I would gladly welcome you to become monthly financial partners with us if the Lord leads you that way. All of our information is on our ministry website: **dwaynenormanministries.org**. But definitely step out in faith and become partners with the ministries God directs you to sow into. In the book of John, the Lord Jesus touched on this principle as well.

"For in this the saying is true: 'One sows and another reaps.'

I sent you to reap that for which you have not labored; others have labored, and you have entered into their labors." (John 4:37, 38)

Amplified Bible says in verse 38, **"I sent you to reap a crop for which you have not toiled. Other men have labored and you have stepped in to reap the results of their work."**

I believe that the Church today will reap the harvest of souls from the seeds of the Gospel sown by men and women of God that went before us. When you are laboring, you are sowing seed. Just like Peter sowed his boat into Jesus' ministry and reaped a great harvest of fish, his partners also reaped the same harvest without sowing the same seed. You could say they reaped from that which they did not labor. What a great blessing God has given us! Can you see that through the partnership we have with other ministries, we can expect to reap the same harvest they are reaping? I believe that God will bless us with the same rewards of which He blesses these ministers for all of the souls they win to the Lord! I believe those who are financial and prayer partners with them shall receive the same rewards, don't you? The grace we are partaking of from these ministries is the results produced from the seeds we have sown into them. Like it was with Peter and his partners, their (the ministries we give to) harvests become our harvests. Isn't sharing and communicating in giving and receiving wonderful?

CHAPTER
9

ENTERING INTO REST
THROUGH THE SEED

It is time for the Church to enter into her rest! It is time for every Believer to experience the rest of God!

"For we who have believed do enter that rest…" (Hebrews 4:3a)
"There remains therefore a rest for the people of God." (Hebrews 4:9)

This rest isn't just for Heaven, but it is for the here and now. Our Heavenly Father has provided for us a way in Christ to daily live at rest despite what's going on in our families, our jobs and this world. This is another area for you and me to take dominion in our lives through the seed. Shadrach, Meshach, and Abed-Nego were at rest while in the middle of a burning, fiery furnace. The lesson to learn here is the fire does not have to be put out to experience God's rest. Your circumstances don't have to change before you can experience God's rest. The economy does not have to change before you can be at rest in the financial area of

135

your life.   Yes, you need to expect those negative circumstances to change, but whether they change or not, you can still live every day in God's supernatural rest.

Faith in God is already our victory that has overcome the world, the devil and all of hell (I John 5:4, 5) even before we see a change in the circumstances! The victory is ours right now! Please remember, when we operate in faith we are not trying to get God to do something for us. He has already done everything for us through Jesus' death and resurrection. Faith is not something we do to get God to respond. Faith is something we do to receive and appropriate what He has already done for us in Christ. So, let's start enjoying all that Jesus finished for us at Calvary! Now, let me show you why we have a right to enter into God's rest.

"But God, who is rich in mercy, because of His great love with which He loved us,

Even when we were dead in trespasses, made us alive together with Christ (by grace you have been saved),

And raised us up together, and <u>made us sit</u> together in the heavenly places in Christ Jesus." (Ephesians 2:4-6)

I want to remind you of some truths in this chapter we should be very developed in. Under the priesthood of the old covenant, the priests never had the privilege to "sit down" from offering sacrifices. To "sit down" symbolizes resting. To "sit down" would mean their work was finished and man's conscience had been cleansed. So, the priests had to offer sacrifices continually day after day because the blood of animals could not cleanse man's conscience (Hebrews 9:6-14). Before Calvary man could not be born again. He could not be made God's righteousness in Christ. The blood of animals only made man ceremonially clean or clean on the outside. But the inside of man was where the problem was, that is why Jesus was born of the virgin Mary and became a man so He could represent the entire human race and fix our problem.

Now here are two questions we need to ask ourselves. Why does the Bible tell us that Jesus sat down when all the other priests did not (Ephesians 2:6; Colossians 3:1; Hebrews 1:3, 13; 10:12)? Why does the Bible tell us that we sat down when Jesus did (Romans 12:5; I Corinthians 12:27; Ephesians 1:23; 5:30; Colossians 1:18)? Once again, what does it mean in these verses when it describes Jesus sitting down? Now this isn't something complex to understand. To sit down simply means to rest doesn't it? And it doesn't always mean to rest because you are tired. Hebrews 4: 4 says:

"For He has spoken in a certain place of the seventh day in this way: 'And God rested on the seventh day from all His works.'"

After God created the worlds He rested, but not because He was tired. He doesn't get tired. He rested because He finished His work. You could even say that He "sat down", so to speak. To sit down is a sign that you are not working but are at rest. Now I know that your job may involve sitting at a computer working, but you are still sitting. When the Bible says that Jesus sat down (Ephesians 1:20) that is referring to the Lord resting. When Jesus sat down at the Father's right hand, we know that all His work was finished. Well what work was that? He came to suffer for man, to fully identify Himself with humanity, to pay our entire penalty for sin, to become a curse for us, to die on the cross, be made alive, to conquer all of hell, to redeem us back to God, to arise from the dead and sit down at the Father's right hand. That is what it means when the Bible says that Jesus sat down! He completed, accomplished and finished everything God sent Him to do, glory to God!

So, why did we sit down in Him? I believe there are two reasons why we sat down: 1. to show that all of our works have been finished. I am not talking about works of faith. I am talking about the works of the flesh, trying to do things our way, trying to redeem ourselves, trying to earn and merit blessings from God. That is what the Lord is talking about in Hebrews 4:10.

"For he who has entered His rest has himself also <u>ceased from his</u> <u>works</u> as God did from His."

He said if you have entered His rest, you have ceased from your works. In other words, one of the evidences that you have entered into God's rest is when you have ceased from your works. If you have been wondering why you are not experiencing the rest of God in your life, this could be the reason, you haven't ceased from your own works. We will never enter into supernatural rest until we totally submit our wills to God and become willing and obedient to say what He tells us to say, and to do what He tells us to do. It sounds like we are getting back to the definition of the word "willing" doesn't it? Being willing has a lot to do with entering God's rest.

Now, there are works that we must show forth to enter into rest. Of course, you know that I am talking about works of faith. Hebrews 3:19 says: **"So we see that they could not enter in because of <u>unbelief</u>."** Hebrews 4:6 says: **"Since therefore it remains that some must enter it, and those to whom it was first preached did not enter because of <u>disobedience</u>."** Unbelief is a lack of faith, which is also disobedience. If we really believe God's Word, we will obey it, and that is operating in faith. Now don't forget that Jesus said releasing our faith, which is how we enter into rest, is the same as sowing a seed (Matthew 17:20).

Therefore, I want you to get a revelation that entering into God's rest comes through sowing seed. When you sow seed into God's Kingdom this way, you are putting works with your faith and expecting to receive freely from God's grace. Let me give you a few examples of works of faith. When you purposely and joyfully bring God your tithes and offerings (not in any way thinking you are buying God's favor) because you love Him, those are works of faith. If it hurts to bend your leg, but you believe that by Jesus' stripes your leg is healed, so you begin to put forth an effort to bend it anyway in Jesus' Name that is a work of faith. When you commit your time to help wherever needed in your church, because you love God, not because you are trying to earn His favor, those are works of faith. You are putting works with your faith when you go to church even though your pastor is out of town. All of these different works of faith are seeds you are sowing on a regular basis.

I told you there were at least two reasons we sat down in Christ. I gave you the first one and now I want to give you the second. When God made us sit down in Christ, He was showing that all Jesus finished at Calvary has been finished for us. Everything Jesus accomplished in His sufferings, death and resurrection wasn't just so He could say that He got His job done. All that He finished and completed was for you and me; it was everything that needed to be finished in our lives which we could not do. We needed to pay our penalty for sin. We could not do that, but He paid it for us. We needed to be redeemed from the curse of the law. We could not redeem ourselves, so He obtained eternal redemption for us. This is what the Lord meant in Ephesians 2:6 when He said that He <u>made</u> us sit. I want to emphasize the word "made". God did all this for us. He made us His sons and daughters, we did not do it. He healed and delivered us, we did not do that either. When I teach on the mystery of Christ (see our book "The Mystery" an in depth study of all God did for us in Christ) I look at seven areas of our redemption: 1. We were crucified with Christ 2. We were buried 3. We died with Him 4. We were made alive with Him 5. We conquered hell with Christ 6. We were raised with Him 7. We were seated in Him.

Because of what God did for us in Christ, we are now living in a new Blood covenant with Him. But I want you to realize that this covenant is an <u>imposed</u> covenant. God <u>made</u> it with us; we did not have any say so in it. I want you to see how the word "made" ties in with the word "imposition". It was an imposition to us, but a very good imposition! An imposition is the action or process of imposing something on someone. The story is told in II Kings chapters 24 and 25 of how King Nebuchadnezzar imposed a covenant on Zedekiah the King of Israel. Nebuchadnezzar set Zedekiah up as king in Jerusalem, but he was really a puppet king. To paraphrase it, if Zedekiah did not accept Nebuchadnezzar's covenant with him then he would be killed. So, you could say he still had a choice in the matter, even though it wasn't a good one, but the best choice was to submit to Nebuchadnezzar's imposition.

God did not come to us before Calvary and discuss with us what His plans were. He did not bring this new covenant in writing to us and ask us to look it over and let Him know if He needed to make any changes in it. He made the covenant through Jesus' shed Blood and told us how we could become part of it and be blessed forever or we could go to hell; the choice was ours. God never asked us if we agreed with everything He was going to do for us at Calvary. He never asked us what we thought of the terms and benefits of His will for us. That is an imposed covenant. Of course this Blood covenant is an awesome and wonderful covenant which we have the privilege to operate in throughout all eternity! I am sure you also know that we got the best end of the deal!! Listen to these verses and you will hear the tone of an imposed covenant.

"Saying, "This is the blood of the covenant which God has <u>commanded</u> you."" (Hebrews 9:20)

"...For there the Lord <u>commanded</u> the blessing - Life forevermore." (Psalm 133:3)

Again, God did not come to us for our recommendation or approval of what He finished for us in Christ. That means we had nothing to do with it. It was all God's idea. He is the one who has made us sit at rest in Christ at His right hand in Heaven. It is already done! That is where you are now! That is your place and position in Christ and you need to get a strong revelation and understanding of that! Sometimes, when I am talking to the Lord I like to say, "Father, you made me to sit at rest in Christ at your very right hand, in your throne room. You did it! I didn't do it! I didn't make me sit! You made me sit! This was all your idea. I had nothing to do with it, but I believe it and I receive it and I praise you for it in Jesus' Name!!"

It is so important that we know that we know that we know what our position or place is in Christ! Out of those seven areas of our redemption covered in the mystery of Christ that I mentioned a page or so back, you will find two different positions that are covered, our position or place before we were made alive and resurrected with Christ and our position after we were made alive. Before we were made alive our place was a place of spiritual death in Adam, where the devil was our god. It was a position of separation from the Father, a place of fear and doubt that was void of rest and peace. After we were made alive or resurrected to newness of life with Christ our position totally changed. <u>You could say that the resurrection gave us a supernatural change of position.</u> The resurrection of Christ can change anyone's position; no matter where that person is in life! The reason God could give us a new position and seat us with Him at His right hand is because He made us alive and resurrected us together with Christ. If He had not changed our spiritual position first, then He could not have seated us in Christ in the Heavenly places. That is why you get to enjoy the place you have with the Father now in Christ. After what you just read, I believe this Scripture in the Old Testament will mean much more to you.

"You will not need to fight in this battle. <u>Position yourselves</u>, stand still and see the salvation of the Lord, who is with you, O Judah and Jerusalem! Do not fear or be dismayed; tomorrow go out against them, for the Lord is with you." (II Chronicles 20:17)

You probably remember the story of how God defended Jehoshaphat and His people from their enemies. The Lord raised up a man that prophesied to them that they would not need to fight in this battle, but that would only happen if they got in the right <u>position</u>. If they did not get in the right position, then they would not experience their victory. I sure hope that you are hearing this! God told them if they positioned themselves correctly then they would not need to fear or be dismayed, and the victory would be theirs. It sounds like God was telling them that they would enter into a supernatural rest if they got in the right place or position doesn't it? It is so vital today that we get established in our place in Christ! I know we are already in Him, but I am talking about becoming more developed in our understanding of what it means to be seated at rest in Christ at God's right hand. <u>A revelation of our spiritual position is what will determine if we are going to experience the rest of God!</u>

Also, please know that everything Jesus accomplished for us and all of the blessings He has given us in our place in Him are included in His grace and because of His grace towards us. So, when we talk about the grace of God, we are talking about every blessing given to us in Christ. You could also say that grace is <u>G</u>od's <u>r</u>iches <u>a</u>t <u>C</u>hrist <u>e</u>xpense. Now, let me tell you from Ephesians 2:7 what our Heavenly Father wants to do for you and me in this life. You could say this is part of the benefit package you have been given because of your new position in Christ.

"That in the ages to come He might show the exceeding riches of His grace in His kindness toward us in Christ Jesus."

It's time now for us to learn how to trust God and receive all that His grace has obtained for us. Galatians 2:21 says:

"I do not set aside the grace of God; for if righteousness comes through the law, then Christ died in vain."

The King James Bible says: **"I do not frustrate the grace of God…"**

God's Word translation says: **"I don't reject God's kindness…"**

Amplified Bible says: **"I do not set aside and invalidate and frustrate and nullify the grace (unmerited favor) of God…"**

Common English Bible says: **"I don't ignore the grace of God…"**

Letters to Street Christians says: **"Don't waste His death. If we could get to the Father by keeping rules, then Jesus hung on that cross for nothing!"**

The William Barclay translation says: **"I am not going to treat the grace of God as if it did not exist…"**

Also, II Corinthians 6:1 says, **"We then, as workers together with Him also plead with you not to receive the grace of God in vain."**

The Apostle Paul is telling us that we need to accept everything that belongs to us in the grace of God, and we need to expect all of these wonderful benefits and blessings to be manifested in our lives. If we don't do that, then we are frustrating and nullifying God's grace in our lives. It is the same as if someone deposited a million dollars in the bank for you and you never make any withdrawals. You would be setting aside, ignoring and invalidating the money that is rightfully yours. Many Christians are doing this right now. They are frustrating the grace of God. They will not release their faith and receive the victory that belongs to them in Christ.

Being under grace (referring to our lives after Calvary) is like having a bank account from God that has an endless supply. When I go to make a withdrawal, I am not trying to get the Lord to put anything in that account, and if my attitude is different than that, then my works are not works of faith but works of the flesh. When I go to make a withdrawal out of that account, I know that what I need is already there, so I am simply going to receive what is already mine by God's grace. I am not trying to get God to do anything for me. The way to make withdrawals from God's grace or out of our Heavenly account has to always be by faith. The Lord told us this in Romans 4:16, **"Therefore it is of faith that it might be according to grace, so that the promise might be sure to all the seed…"**

"Through whom also <u>we have access by faith into this grace</u> in which we stand, and rejoice in hope of the glory of God." (Romans 5:2)

It takes faith to believe that God has already done everything for us in Christ. If we really believe that everything is finished by God's grace, then we will be at rest. If we really believe we already have eternal life in Christ then we will be at rest about our salvation, and we will never wonder if we are truly saved. If we really believe that by Jesus' stripes we are healed, then we will be at rest where healing is concerned. We will have a confident expectation that our healing will be manifested. If we really believe what the Lord said about seedtime and harvest, then after we have sown our seed we will be at rest about our harvest coming to pass. We will keep praising the Lord and giving Him all the glory until we reap our harvest.

What is the connection between the rest of God and His grace? God's grace reveals to us all that He has given us in Christ. His rest reminds us that we don't have to work up anything to receive what is already ours in His grace. We don't have to pray in tongues loud and fast, we don't have to grit our teeth and get all tight and tense to receive what already belongs to us. If I bought you a car and gave it to you as a gift, what would you have to do to receive it? Just say thank you, I receive it. That's it! We must get our minds renewed to the Word of God concerning all that God finished for us in Christ. Walking by faith is how God's people walked in the old covenant, and that is how we walk in the new covenant as well, but there is a difference though in the attitude of faith after Calvary compared to the attitude of faith before Calvary. Before Jesus shed His Blood and redeemed us, the attitude of faith was, if I sow my seed or release my faith, then God will do something for me. In the world it is called "Quid pro quo"; if I do something for you then you have to do something for me.

The thinking was, if I can do something first, then I can get God to move and do something for me. So, the attitude was, what do I need to do to get the Lord to move on my behalf? Under grace we should not think that way. We don't sow our seed or release our faith for God to do something for us. We operate in faith to receive what is already ours in Christ. Our spiritual attitude should be, since God has already finished everything for me, then I am not sowing my seed to get Him to do something, but simply to appropriate what He has already done. We already have the victory. We don't pray for God to give us the victory. We pray every day from a place of victory. We don't pray for God to heal us because He did that for us through the thirty-nine stripes of Jesus. We reach out by faith and receive our healing and praise Him for it in Jesus' Name.

Are you seeing this? This attitude is exactly what I believe the Apostle Paul was referring to in Ephesians 4:23, **"And be renewed in the spirit of your mind."** When it comes to our finances in this new covenant, we sow our seed from a place of financial victory. We are not sowing to get financial victory. I know that in the natural realm you may need a lot of money, but in Christ, God has already made you financially wealthy and rich. That is part of the supernatural rest of God. You have to see (through your eyes of faith) all your bills paid off and plenty of money in the bank before you see it with your natural eyes. Then from that attitude of faith you sow your tithes and offerings expecting to experience supernatural money, expecting to experience the financial blessings which are already yours. Let's look again at what the Lord Jesus said in Mark 4:26, 27.

"And He said, "The kingdom of God is as if a man should scatter seed on the ground,

And should <u>sleep</u> by night and rise by day, and the seed should sprout and grow, he himself does not know how."

Jesus said after the man sows his seed he can go to sleep or you could say that he can <u>rest</u>. I believe the Lord wants us to understand that the way to enter into His rest is through the seed. I know you may be thinking right now, well according to Hebrews chapter 4 we are to enter into rest through our faith. That is one hundred percent correct, but remember our faith is a seed we sow. Matthew 17:20 says:

"So Jesus said to them, "Because of your unbelief; for assuredly, I say to you, if you have <u>faith as a</u> mustard <u>seed</u>, you will say to this mountain, 'Move from here to there,' and it will move; and nothing will be impossible for you."

When we release our faith by saying, we are sowing seed for a harvest. The harvest is defined by what we are saying, and the harvest is in that seed. What you say will be your harvest, if you believe in your heart that it will come to pass. Well, where does the rest come in? God guaranteed us in Genesis 8:22 that while the earth remains seedtime and harvest will not cease. In other words, when you have seedtime, you can always expect to have harvest time. In the financial realm, when you mix your faith with your tithes and offerings and sow them into God's Kingdom business, you can then rest; you can take a nap like Jesus did because you have absolute confidence that your harvest will be manifested. In Mark 4:35-41, Jesus told His disciples they were going to cross over to the other side of the sea, and then He lay down and went to sleep. He sowed His faith by saying what He believed and expected to come to pass. After He sowed His seed, you could say he entered into rest about His trip. Soon a bad storm came up and started filling the boat with water, but Jesus wasn't stressed or worried at all, He was still sleeping. He was at rest!

Regardless of the circumstances, Jesus knew that He would reap the harvest from the seed He sowed when He got in the boat. The disciples were so worried and afraid (they were not at rest because they were not in faith) they woke up Jesus and He ended up rebuking the storm and it immediately stopped. This is how you enter into God's supernatural rest. It works the same way for your finances. You know that you are a faithful tither and giver. You know that you have sown your seed in obedience to God's Word; therefore, you can rest. You are at rest about your harvest. You have total confidence it will come to pass. You are not worried about your financial situation anymore because you have plenty of seed in the ground. To have plenty of seed in the ground means lots of harvests!

Now, you go through each day expecting to experience supernatural money in Jesus' Name! You know that your financial harvests will come to pass because God's Word is true and you have sown your seed! Once again, you have seed in the ground. You have released your faith through your financial seed to receive the financial blessings which are already yours in Christ. Here is something I like to say, "I have seed in the ground and it's producing for me every day!" This works the same way to enter into rest for your healing. When you believe and declare that by Jesus' stripes you are healed, you are sowing the seed of your faith for a harvest of healing. You can then rest knowing that your healing must come to pass. Sowing your faith as a seed works the same in every realm. Can you see how you are entering into rest through the seed? Do you remember what God said about His Word in Isaiah 55:10, 11?

"For as the rain comes down, and the snow from heaven, and do not return there, but water the earth, and make it bring forth and bud, that it may give seed to the sower, and bread to the eater,
So shall My word be that goes forth from My mouth; it shall not return to Me void, but it shall

**accomplish what I please, and it shall prosper in the
thing for which I sent it."**

God is comparing His Word to rain or water
(Ephesians 5:26) coming down and watering the earth
so that a harvest comes forth. When God speaks His
Word, and He speaks it through you and me, it will not
return to Him void (empty or without fruit) but it will
accomplish what it is sent to do; in other words, it will
become a prosperous seed. Words are containers, they
can contain faith and peace, or fear and doubt. You
decide. When you got saved, you entered into rest
spiritually didn't you? Before you were born again you
did not have any peace within. Well what did you do
to enter into spiritual rest and peace? You received
Jesus as your Lord and Savior didn't you? How did
you do that? By sowing your faith as a seed, you acted
on Romans 10:9 and confessed Jesus as your Lord and
believed in your heart that God raised Him from the
dead. What happened then? You reaped the harvest of
salvation, and you entered into spiritual rest.

How would you enter into rest for your physical
body? You would do it the same way, through sowing
a seed (the seed of your faith). Disease in the body is
actually dis-ease. If your body has a disease, then it's
not at ease or rest is it? Therefore, physically speaking,
you need to enter into rest. Obviously, when your
healing is totally manifested you will be experiencing

the fullness of rest, but there is also a rest we can experience before our healing or miracle is completely manifested. There is a rest of faith that comes through knowing that your healing will come to pass before you feel it. The same is true in the financial realm. If you are believing God for a financial miracle and you have already sown your seed for it, then you should enter into rest that your harvest will come pass.

When a farmer sows his corn seed he enters into a rest that comes from knowing that if you have seedtime you will have a harvest time. While he is waiting for his corn harvest to come forth, he does not fear and worry all day that it might not happen. He has entered into rest even before his harvest is manifested, but he entered into this rest only after he sowed his seed. After he sowed his seed, he knows that he set the law of sowing and reaping into motion, and it has to work. He can go home and go to sleep knowing that he will reap his harvest. So, can you see that he actually entered into rest as soon as he sowed his seed? As soon as you give your tithes and offerings, and I am talking about giving in faith knowing that God has already made you financially prosperous through Jesus' death and resurrection (II Corinthians 8:9), then you can go take a nap knowing that your harvests will come to pass.

Let's daily continue to remind ourselves that God has made us to sit in Christ at rest in His grace at His right hand in Heaven! That is our place and position in Christ and it's from that place we live and move and have our being on the earth! You could say that we are living down here from up there, so we are not praying for God to open up the heavens for us, but we are continually living and ministering to others under an open Heaven! We are the Blessed of the Lord and a great Blessing to others!!

About the Author

Dwayne Norman is a 1978 graduate of Christ For The Nations Bible Institute in Dallas, Texas. He spent 3 years witnessing to prostitutes and pimps in the red light district of Dallas, and another 3 years ministering as a team leader in the Campus Challenge ministry of Dr. Norvel Hayes. He was ordained by Pastor Buddy and Pat Harrison of Faith Christian Fellowship in Tulsa, Oklahoma in September 1980. He also taught evangelism classes several times at Dr. Hayes' Bible school in Tennessee.

Soon the Lord led him to go on the road ministering. He ministers powerfully on soul winning, and on how God wants to use all Believers in demonstrating His Kingdom not just in Word but also in Power!

He teaches with clarity, the work that God accomplished for all believers in Christ from the cross to the throne, and the importance of this revelation to the church for the fulfillment of Jesus' commission to make disciples of all nations.

He strongly believes that we are called to do the works Jesus did and greater works in His Name, not just in church but especially in the market place. As a result, Dwayne experiences many healing miracles in his services, arms and legs growing out, as well as other miracles.

He and his wife Leia travel and teach Supernatural Evangelism and train Believers in who they are in Christ and how to operate in their ministries.

To inquire for meetings with Dwayne & Leia Norman, please contact them at:

Dwayne & Leia Norman
124 Evergreen Court
Mt. Sterling, KY 40353

(859) 351-6496
dwayne7@att.net
Web: www.dwaynenormanministries.org

Contact Dwayne to order his other books and products:

The Mystery DVD's (12 hours) $50.00
The Mystery (book) $12.00
The Mystery Study Guide $10.00
The Awesome Power in the
Message of the Cross $10.00
Your Beginning with God $10.00
The Law of the Spirit
of Life in Christ Jesus $10.00
Demonstrating God's Kingdom $10.00

www.ingramcontent.com/pod-product-compliance
Lightning Source LLC
La Vergne TN
LVHW051557080426
835510LV00020B/3013